The Appraisal
Check List

The Institute of Management (IM) is at the forefront of management development and best management practice. The Institute embraces all levels of management from students to chief executives. It provides a unique portfolio of services for all managers, enabling them to develop skills and achieve management excellence.

If you would like to hear more about the benefits of membership, please write to Department P, Institute of Management, Cottingham Road, Corby NN17 1TT.

This series is commissioned by the Institute of Management Foundation.

SMARTER SOLUTIONS

The people pack

The Appraisal Check List

How to help your team get the results you both want

BRIAN WATLING

London · New York · Toronto · Sydney · Tokyo · Singapore
Madrid · Mexico City · Munich · Paris

PEARSON EDUCATION LIMITED

Head Office:
Edinburgh Gate
Harlow CM20 2JE
Tel: +44 (0)1279 623623
Fax: +44 (0)1279 431059

London Office:
128 Long Acre, London WC2E 9AN
Tel: +44 (0)207 447 2000
Fax: +44 (0)207 240 5771
www.business-minds.com

First published in Great Britain in 1995

© Brian Watling 2000

ISBN 0 273 64483 1

British Library Cataloguing in Publication Data
A CIP catalogue record for this book can be obtained from the British Library.

10 9 8 7 6 5 4 3 2 1

Typeset by Northern Phototypesetting Co. Ltd, Bolton ,
Printed and bound in Great Britain by Biddles Ltd, Guildford and King's Lynn

The Publishers' policy is to use paper manufactured from sustainable forests.

Contents

CONTENTS

Introduction

You do not have to read the whole book to get really valuable information and direction about appraisals. Each chapter is a mini-book in itself because each chapter has been written to stand alone, therefore the reader can identify those topics most needed or those of most interest, and go straight to the text dealing with them. If, however, you are a manager who would like to comprehend the wider picture of appraisals – what needs to be in place in the company to put an appraisal system into operation and how to go about it – then the whole book will be valuable reading.

Once read, it can become a ready reference manual, an off-the-shelf, do-it-yourself workbook that will quickly remind or instruct you in the simple elements of conducting successful appraisals. No matter what stage you are at, a new manager about to conduct your first appraisal, or a seasoned and experienced manager perhaps seeking a more effective way of conducting appraisals, this book is for you. If you do not know how to conduct appraisals now, you will when you have read this book. If you do not know how to put an appraisal process into your company now, you will when you have read the book. To help you, you will find bullet points at the beginning of each chapter identifying, in broad terms, the content of the chapter; at the conclusion of each chapter there is a bullet point summary. The book contains golden rules of dos and don'ts, anecdotes to illustrate clearly the principle or practice being discussed, and illustrations to show how things should be done. There are check lists which will help you to remember the processes and, all in all, you will find this is a practical book, one that has been written from experience to give practical guidance. There is no jargon used and you will find that each chapter is an interesting and practical guide to establishing principles and processes that will ensure that the appraisals you conduct will be meaningful, effective and a pleasant experience for all concerned.

CHAPTER ONE

Why performance management?

In this chapter we examine:

- The benefits of performance management
- The importance of setting objectives
- Communication with the team
- The right people in the rght job

Performance management has to be one of the most exciting opportunities that any organisation has to reach goals, achieve objectives and raise standards. Why is it then that so many companies fail to implement it? Or why is it that so many performance management processes are poorly managed in themselves? Why is it that appraisals, performance management, call it what you will, still provoke widespread fear, suspicion and cynicism?

Of all the questions connected with performance management or appraisals, *Why have them?* is still amongst the questions most often asked. Having said this, it is worth noting that those who ask this question are not always looking for a sensible answer, in fact to get one would mean that they would have to question their attitude and why they asked the question in the first place. This is because so often the question is asked sarcastically, or with more than a hint of cynicism. Those who ask this way consider any measurement of their performance to be an imposition, a nuisance or an infringement of their rights, and because of this attitude they fail to benefit from all the positive objectives behind giving and receiving feedback. These people ask the question not to get a sensible answer, but to reinforce their opinion that any measurement of performance is a waste of time.

Sometimes the question is asked out of genuine concern; there is fear and deep apprehension about *who* is doing the measuring and any *hidden agenda* they may have. More often than not this is because the performance management process is welded to the pay review, therefore the real concern is that the whole process, including those carrying out the process, may not reflect unbiased, objective and fair assessment of individual performance.

The previous two paragraphs have highlighted the real reasons why anyone would question the value of performance management, but they don't answer the opening questions. To answer these we may have to conclude that perhaps the benefits of performance management are not known or fully understood. So, let us look at the benefits – to the organisation and to the individual – and let us see if we can ensure that there is no justification for any organisation or individual to do anything other than use performance management to maximum effectiveness.

The benefits of performance management

- Keeps the vision focused and in place
- Sets performance standards and objectives across the organisation
- Offers two-way feedback on performance and issues
- Identifies training and development needs
- Strengthens and builds relationships
- Maximises people potential
- Can provide a database of people skills for succession planning
- Keeps the organisation competitive
- Aids morale (only when meaningful)

We will look at these benefits in turn, and elaborate on each of them in order to get a more complete understanding of exactly what the benefits are, and how when they are applied, they can make performance management a more meaningful process.

Keeps the Vision focused and in place

All performance should be evaluated against the goal of making the company vision a reality. This ensures that all employees understand that the contribution they make has a much wider implication than just the immediate job they do. It also ensures that the organisation is broadly going in 'the same direction'. Having and keeping in mind the 'bit picture' ensures that individual empires are not created; it also ensures that cooperation between colleagues and departments is easier to maintain. Richard Branson's Virgin enterprise is a good example of how the vision is created, communicated and maintained, and how a corporate identity is adopted throughout an organisation.

Sets performance standards and objectives across the organisation

The assumption being made here is that wherever one may go in an organisation, there will be standardisation of the practices and values the organisation embraces. Whilst the standards of performance will be set for each job, there will be codes of conduct that cut across all departments. These codes of conduct represent how the vision is put into place and operated; they dictate how the organisation will 'do its business'. No matter where one works, or for whom in the organisation, performance management processes are designed to ensure that there is continuity and standardisation of approach to measuring individual contribution.

Offers two-way feedback on performance and issues

The opportunity to have frank and open discussion on one's performance, including feedback to the person managing, is an integral part of performance management. Realising that there will be an understandable reluctance to be open with a manager who is perceived to be over critical or downright belligerent, and if we can keep politics out of the equation, performance management is a good opportunity to identify stumbling blocks and to agree the way forward.

Identifies training and development needs

This is one of the fundamental objectives of performance management/appraisals. When this objective is given the priority it deserves, there is a real opportunity to see performance management as a positive and motivational experience. The application of this objective demonstrates commitment on the behalf of management to developing the organisation's greatest asset, namely its people. Using performance management to identify training and development needs means that the organisation can be proactive as well as reactive; it means that career planning and succession planning can become a reality.

Strengthens and builds relationships

Communication has always been the basis of any successful relationship, and performance management is all about communication. Whether performance has been good or needing serious improvement, having a process to monitor and give feedback, provides the opportunity to build strong business relationships. This is more obvious when managers are trained in the delivery of performance management skills and processes.

Maximises people potential

The whole implication of the words 'performance management' is that potential is identified and developed. Potential isn't just doing more, it is working smarter and giving people the opportunity to learn and acquire new skills. Using an objective approach to identifying potential, and applying objectivity to developing people, makes training and development much more exciting.

Can provide a database of people skills for succession planning

If the organisation has the mind and will, as well as the technical ability, then a database can be created storing the development progress of each member of staff. When the performance management process includes the competencies for each job, and these competencies have been benchmarked, then the monitoring of performance against these benchmarks becomes a relatively simple process. The database allows the cross-referencing of people skills and the job requirements and is an excellent tool for succession planning, giving the organisation the opportunity to promote from within.

Keep the organisation competitive

Job stability in the sense that a person works for the same organisation for 20 years or more is a thing of the past. It is widely accepted that the new generations of workers are likely to move several times during their working life in order to progress their career. This means that employability is going to be more closely aligned with skill level, and developing the workforce a must to stay ahead of the competition, or at least to keep up with the competition. Of course it also means that those organisations that offer real training and development will attract the right people.

Aids morale (only when meaningful)

Performance management that is seen and appreciated as a means for personal development, where honesty and frankness can be applied to the building of sound relationships, and where working for an organisation is hard, enjoyable and rewarding, will create an environment where morale flourishes and achievement is assured. Performance management is very much about getting the best out of people and helping people produce their best and realise their potential. People who feel good about themselves produce good results.

The above are very good benefits aren't they? Certainly, too good to ignore. Every organisation, and every individual, can really benefit from performance management provided the process is properly implemented and monitored, and the managers properly trained. Another key element is to ensure that as far as possible, the right person is doing the right job.

Apart from its many other fine qualities, one of the things that really impressed me about the film 'Ben Hur' was the scene that shows Charlton Heston as Judah Ben Hur returning to his homeland. In this scene he arrives at the camp of an arab nobleman and watches the preparation of a team of horses for a forthcoming chariot race. Having been a champion chariot racer himself in Rome, Judah is able to critique the performance of the horses and suggest that to produce a winning team the positions of the horses needed to change, to maximize individual strengths. Needless to say his advice was taken and he went on to drive the team to victory. My observation is this: if every team were organised this way, if every position on the team was filled with the right person in the right job, then winning would become a way of life. Of course it is not easy; if it were everyone would be doing it and doing it continuously. This book is all about getting it right every time and keeping it right all the time.

Knowing who is the 'right person' starts with knowing 'what is the job'. In other words, if you don't know what the expectation is, i.e. what the job is supposed to produce, you can hardly start to match the skills of those applying for the job with the skills necessary to do the job. While this may sound obvious, there is evidence in abundance of 'square pegs in round holes' throughout industry. One of the principle causes for this situation lies in the fact that we are pretty good at setting academic qualifications for the jobs we want to fill, but when it comes down to identifying inter-personal skills, organisational skills, leadership skills etc., there seems to be a lot lacking. If the team is to 'run together' so to speak, then academic qualifications must balance with the 'people' skills to ensure that the team not only *can* do the job, but that they *will* do the job, and in doing it will generate enthusiasm, energy and synergy.

Testing leadership

Let me illustrate my point with an experience. I had taken a group of managers to an army camp to put them through some command tasks, the purpose being to determine the depth of their leadership skills and to test their ability to act as team members. Imagine if you can, ten very strong-willed and self-opinionated individuals with very different styles of management, and yet each one running successful teams. If you have been subjected to army leadership training through the use of command tasks, then you will know that each exercise has a number of items and the members of the team have to go over various obstacles in a set period of time. What you may not know is the fact that the observers are more interested in how the task is accomplished, rather than the fact that it is accomplished.

But to return to the story, I watched with interest as each member of the team took his turn to lead the team through the command task. I saw each one, bar one, fall into the trap of assuming that getting the job done was all that mattered. Every leader who took this stance failed to complete the task, both in the time allowed and in getting the equipment and team members safely over the obstacle. Time was lost as team members reacted to unpopular styles and either argued or went into moods. Oftimes the wrong people pushed themselves to the fore to take on chores others were clearly better suited for. At best, two or three members of the team would be carried along with plain enthusiasm, while the others would be either uncooperative or would do just enough to satisfy a loose description of cooperation. Except, as I have said, one particular manager who handled things very differently. The first thing that impressed me about his approach was his willingness to listen very carefully to all the instructions regarding the objective and its accomplishment. In other words, he took time to understand what the job entailed and what successful completion of the job would look like. He asked questions to get clarity and clearly identified the parameters within which he was to work. Then he went to his team and explained to them all that he had learned, and tested their understanding. He invited input from the team asking for suggestions as to how the objective should be reached and invited individuals to identify where they thought they might make the most positive contribution. When the team finally attempted the task, not only did they achieve the objective of getting both equipment and team members over the obstacle, but each member of the team made a positive contribution to the success. His evaluation by the officers assessing his performance was that he had high levels of leadership and motivation skills.

This true experience creates a good model and produces a useful process from which some parallels can be drawn. Refer to Fig. 1, which illustrates the process, as we examine each step and get some understanding of the principles upon which it is based.

1 Management knows the overall objective

2 This is communicated to team leaders

3 It is then communicated to the team

4 The team is invited to contribute to the planning

5 Individual strengths are identfied

6 The team accomplishes the task

Figure 1

_____ 1 _____

Management knows the overall objective

Not so obvious as it may first appear is the need for the company, i.e. senior management, to know what the objective of the company is. So often there appears to be a 'lack of direction from the top', and when that 'lack of direction' manifests itself, it is usually evidence that those leading the company have lost sight of 'why the company is in business', and it is never enough to say 'to make a profit' – there is so much more to it than this. Strategic planning covers how the objectives are to be achieved and involves a statement of intent or a mission statement, so let us consider this.

While many of us will not be involved in the strategic planning of company object-ives, it is very useful to know how this is done. Often the overall objectives are published in a *mission statement*. This is a brief statement outlining *why* the company is in business and *how* it conducts its business. The statement is influenced by four criteria: the **vision** of the company, the **objectives** of the company, the **values** of the company and company **strategy**. The following is a typical example of a company mission statement:

> Our mission is to commit ourselves to doing all we can to ensure that superior performance associated with quality is our normal behaviour.

Although a simple statement, it does communicate the vision and the values of the company as well as setting the broad background for objectives and the strategy by which this vision will be realised. I believe this principle applies to everything we do, or it can do, and when it does we start to enjoy constant success. It gives a sense of purpose and direction and, more importantly, allows everyone in the organisation to plot progress against a known statement of intent.

Going back to our story, can you see how this illustrates the principle in the most simple of examples? The company is represented by the army officers who quite clearly had a vision of what was to be accomplished and how it was to be done. As this was not a 'success at any price' scenario, there were values to consider and, of course, there were a number of objectives to be accomplished, all of which were communicated to the team leader. What they didn't do was tell each team leader precisely how to get the job done. This was left to individual initiative and assessment, which of course is what we want, and this will happen when individual team members know the overall objectives and are given the freedom to use their own initiative to get the job done.

_____ 2/3 _____

This is communicated to team leaders, who communicate it to the team

Steps two and three in the process are all about communication and the need for everyone to know and understand at least two basic things:

1 What the job is.

2 How their contribution helps to achieve the overall objective.

Much more will be said on these two topics in the next chapter, but the subject of communication should be expanded here.

The art of communication

Some years ago, while working for an engineering company as an apprentice, a fellow apprentice came to me with a worried look on his face. It appeared that he had been left an instruction that was ambiguous and unclear ordering him to carry out some work which was running to a tight schedule. Adding to his problem was the fact that a management meeting had been called and no one was available to give clarification as to what was wanted. This is how the instruction read: 'The current pattern we use is slightly wrong and needs to be altered. You can do this by looking in bay 10 tray 4. If it is not there find out where it is, however it is important that you get 10 moulds cast before noon to meet the deadline.' Whatever you make of this message, the manager was trying to convey the importance of casting 10 moulds before noon to meet the deadlines. However you can see why my colleague was so perturbed. His confusion led to him not only failing to find the new pattern, which is what the manager was asking him to do, but also in failing to get the moulds made and casted, which was critical, because he believed that to mould and cast the old pattern was not what was wanted.

Has this ever happened to you? Have you ever asked a subordinate what they were doing, because whatever they were doing did not in the slightest way resemble what you had asked them to do? Yes? I wonder how many times, and I wonder if the reason lay behind your failure to communicate clearly what was wanted. One of the big problems with communication is the fact that we know what we mean and so we assume that everyone else knows what we mean. If we are to avoid confusion, resulting in lost production, frustration, poor morale and possibly staff turnover, we must learn to be good communicators, and we start by being good listeners.

In the financial services industry there is a sales process which comprises two steps closely allied to good communication: the first is referred to as 'the opening' and the second as 'the close'. The step describing *opening* is very much about being a good conversationalist, making people feel at ease and listening for opportunities to present your product. To watch a good opener is an education in people skills and the art of communication. Often these very skilled people are accused of being able to 'talk the hind legs off a donkey'. Actually they are brilliant listeners. Couple this with the skill of *closing* and you now have a communicator extraordinaire. For remembering all they have heard, these skilful people then match their products with client needs and get a natural agreement. They do this by learning and obeying some very important **golden rules** which come out of the word communicate. Here they are:

C	–	Clearly state your need/instruction
O	–	Open discussion
M	–	Minimise misunderstanding
M	–	Make notes
U	–	Umpire the message
N	–	Never assume
I	–	Impel listening
C	–	Chase response
A	–	Action
T	–	Touch base regularly
E	–	Evaluate progress

We started this section by talking about the importance of communicating the objective to the team and developed this into some basic principles governing communication. Let us conclude steps two and three by reiterating, **make sure that every member of the team has a clear and concise understanding of what is to be accomplished, and the importance of each individual's contribution to the success of the team.**

_____ 4 _____

The team is invited to contribute to the planning

I remember well working for a manager who would say regularly, 'When I want your opinion I'll give it to you', and he meant it. Here was a manager who felt it was his job to tell, tell and tell and upward communication was not wanted or appreciated. The result was that nobody under him developed. Those who enjoyed being told constantly what and how to do the job remained in his section and never got the opportunity to progress; those of us who were looking to be appreciated for initiative and for creativity couldn't get away from him fast enough. On another occasion I witnessed a manager say to a new recruit, 'There are only three ways of doing this job: my way, my way, and my way'. Fortunately he went on to explain that until the recruit had learned the basic way of doing things, his discipline was to do things the manager's way. Then he would be given the freedom to use his own initiative.

I believe this is fair enough, but there must come a time when each member of the team is given an opportunity, even an ongoing one, to make suggestions for getting the job done more efficiently and more effectively. It is also worth remembering that people have a pretty good idea of what they are good at and what they are not good at, so inviting suggestions from them as to how they see their contributions helping the team to success makes good sense.

The power of teamwork

Some years ago I ran a residential managers course at Billesley Manor near Stratford-upon-Avon, and the first activity I got the managers involved in after setting up teams was a treasure hunt. It was a simple exercise made up of a cross between simple general knowledge questions concerning the manor and its history and layout, and the surrounding countryside. Although it was not strictly a timed activity and no points were earned for the team who completed it first, I was very much interested in the way the teams organised themselves. For example, one of the teams flew around dragging the slowest member of the team behind and not allowing him to make any positive contribution at all. The other team, however, sat around the table, discussed each clue, decided their strategy, which was to split into two groups (one to cover the manor, the other to cover outside), then decided through discussion who was to do what. They quickly moulded themselves into a formidable team that was to excel in all the team activities throughout the week.

This concept can and should be taken into the workplace because, just like my teams on the course who did not choose one another, teams at work often have to discover for themselves each other's strengths and weaknesses and come to terms with difficult personalities. But when they do and when each member of the team feels that they can contribute something through discussion, then you have *synergy*. It is worth expanding on synergy for a moment, because, in essence, it is very powerful and when you achieve it you have a team which constantly knows what success feels like.

A simple definition for synergy is this, that the whole team is greater than any individual member of it. There are no 'prima donnas'; everyone has a contribution to make, without which the team would be both poorer and less effective. Synergy leads to openness, creativity and seeing opportunity instead of obstacle. Weaknesses become strengths because instead of seeing barriers or frustration you see new horizons. But it can only happen when individuals feel part of the team and when individuals feel they *are* the team. You start by encouraging each member to contribute to discussion and to make suggestions. This, then, is step four in our process.

_____ 5 _____

Individual strengths are identified

Step five almost takes us back to my opening remarks concerning 'Ben Hur' and knowing where to place each horse to bring about the best results. In fact, knowing strengths and weaknesses opens up enormous opportunity for development and progress. I have stated previously that most people know their own strengths and weaknesses and, at the risk of contradicting myself, I am now going to say that it is equally true that we are often bound by misperception. What I mean is that we are often capable of that which we think we are not, but because we think we can't, we can't. This means that the true leader must recognise potential and misplaced limitations. It also means that he/she must be aware of the power of peer pressure, because we may find ourselves doing something we are very uncomfortable with, but, because we do not want to let down the team, we do it anyway.

Let me cite two examples which illustrate the need for team leaders and managers to be aware of the power of peer pressure and to be sensitive when identifying strengths and weaknesses. Both examples happened while I was running management training courses. The first was in Cambridgeshire and again involved the managers being arranged into two teams of five members.

Peer pressure

The course was very intensive and so to give the teams an opportunity to exercise their bodies as well as their brains, on Wednesday of the week I had arranged a boat race on the river Cam. There was a general air of enthusiasm and anticipation coming from both teams, but it was brought to my attention that one team member was disturbed. When I spoke to him I discovered that he was petrified of water – some early experiences had left him with a real dread and not only could he not swim, but he never went on water, even in boats, if he could avoid it. Of course I immediately withdrew his obligation to participate, but this only worsened the situation because he was by now really caught up in the team spirit and he did not want to let the team down. After much discussion and planning, I was able to arrange a life jacket for him and he did participate, and to his credit he overcame his initial fear and went on to enjoy the race. I am certain that were he not participating as a team member, he would not even have got into the boat that day, and I saw again the power of peer pressure. I shall always be grateful to the team leader who was smart enough to find out about his team members and to recognise potential danger, but who also made sure that this particular team member made a valuable contribution to the success of the team on this occasion.

In the second example, a team member was not so fortunate, although the story has a happy ending. Perhaps I ought to point out before continuing with this example that my approach to team exercises is a very responsible one. I make sure participants know before attending the courses the nature of the activities. I also require from them acceptance in writing to participate and I do state very clearly that no one has to do anything that they do not feel comfortable with. However, on just these two occasions peer pressure did lead individuals to attempt activities that they would not normally participate in. But on with the second example.

I had arranged for a group of managers to attend an army officer training camp where a number of exercises were to take place. One of these exercises involved overcoming fear and each team member was asked to identify from a list of six the task they most feared. The officer in charge then determined that this was the task that the individual would complete in order to help overcome that fear. One manager not only voiced his fears but was adamant that he would not participate, and this was, of course, totally acceptable. However, the peer pressure then started to work and he became tormented as to what he should do. After constant assurance that he need not participate, he decided that he must because he did not want to let down his team. His fear was the fireman's pole which was some 30 feet above ground level. Each team member was to climb up some scaffolding to a platform where they would be instructed on how to launch themselves on to the pole, and the correct way to descend. We watched him closely and he was accompanied each step of the way. When it came to his turn, his apprehension was obvious but, overcoming his fear, he launched himself on to the pole and then froze. With coaxing and constant assurance he began slowly to lower himself down the pole. However, with about 20 feet still to go, he suddenly let go and plummeted to the ground below. He was not seriously injured, although of course he could have been. Again I saw the power of peer pressure and the need for team leaders to be very careful when identifying the strengths of the team.

To relate this to the office is easy. There have been many occasions in departmental meetings or sectional meetings when I have seen individuals, not wishing to be seen as non-team members, make commitments, take on responsibilities or agree deadlines which they then fail to keep. This is not always because of a lack of ability, but it is very often because they think they are better or more organised than they really are. Pressured to take part in the team to ensure that the team succeeds, so often they become the reason why the team fails.

In the workplace there are a number of tools that can be used to identify and measure strengths and weaknesses, and these can contribute positively if they are used correctly and kept in perspective. I do not believe there is a real substitute for working with a person and discovering for ourselves the strengths and weaknesses of an individual, but there are some useful tools to help us make our evaluation both objective and correct. Criteria-based interviewing is the best method I have found for getting closest to the real thing. It provides real evidence (or indeed the lack of it) which will support whether a skill is both known and used, and at what level the skill is being used. Chapter 3 deals with the process of criteria-based interviews and will identify how this skill enhances the skill of appraising.

The following is a list of tools or activities that will help identify individual skills. I will make some comment about each one in order to help the reader determine the value of each; however I have found that whether or not something has value depends largely on the way it is used, and the belief in the tool or activity that the user displays. The list is not exhaustive, just a few I have used.

- Psychological profiling and testing
- Business games/case studies
- Role plays
- Leadership exercises
- Interview guides (especially criteria-based interviews)
- Appraisals (especially criteria-based appraisals)
- Assessment centres

Psychological profiling

There are a number of excellent profiling tools available. I will mention two in particular only because I have used them very successfully. The first is the PPA marketed by Thomas International. I have used this to help me with the selection of candidates in job interviews. Very broadly, it measures aptitude and, through the use of a question-naire, makes individuals choose between words that might describe the way they behave in a work environment. It then interprets the responses and identifies person-ality traits such as dominance, influence, etc. It is intended as a guide and should be used with other selection tools before drawing any firm conclusions. I know that Thomas International also market a computer-based programme and further psycho-logical programmes to aid in identifying individual skills.

The other profiling process that I have used is the one marketed by the Psychological Research Foundation and run by Don Warley. Again this measures the personality profile by interpreting a number of tests and measuring instruments, and again encourages the user to view the findings as additional information.

I believe in psychological profiling because it gives a very sound starting point and provides data that you can attempt to prove or disprove. It also gives you an insight into the way people are likely to behave, their styles and likely reactions to situations and people.

Psychological tests

Psychological tests tend to go further than profiling and consist of a number of tests covering mathematical abilities, the ability to form opinions or to interpret information in order to make decisions, and many other disciplines. These tests take place over a number of days depending on what is required. The psychological test that I experi-enced lasted one day and was designed to determine whether or not I had the makings of an executive. Large corporations use this means of testing ability and skill. You will also find that many assessment centres use similar tools for testing and evaluation.

Business games

The reason these are called business games is because the exercises are designed to represent the type of scenario you are likely to experience in the workplace. There are literally hundreds of business games and probably as many companies marketing them. I have used them on courses with good results because they range from simple 'getting to know you' activities to the more sophisticated ones which test time management skills, self-discipline, financial planning skills, etc.

Case studies

I have separated case studies from business games because they can be used to suit each individual situation. For example, I can create a case study to test individuals in the financial services industry, or I can create one to test individuals in the retail trade; I can invent a case study based on my own experience, or I can use a 'real life' experience to test individuals. In fact, some of the most powerful case studies I have used have been actual cases where both the circumstances and the outcomes were known to me. It certainly makes the comparisons between what was done and what those being tested propose should be done very interesting. Of course it also tells you very quickly whether the style or method to be used would fit your situation or environment.

Role plays

This is an excellent way to test a skill and is very close to the real thing. For example, suppose I wanted to test your ability as a decision-maker. How easy it is to slip into a role play by saying, 'Ok, I'll be a colleague who has come to you with a problem that you should deal with,' (I would then state the problem, making it relevant to the work situation). 'How will you deal with it?' Once the conversation has started you can stay in the role as long as you wish, testing not just one skill but any others that you might want to look for.

Leadership exercises

I have already cited a few examples of where I have used this type of exercise in setting up teams and testing individual's leadership abilities. I have always found the Army an excellent source for both testing and teaching leadership skills. Other excellent training sources in leadership skills are the Outward Bound centres, because again they use real situations to test not only skills, but also the style and manner in which they are applied.

Interview guides and appraisals

I have put these two together because most of what I want to say about them will appear in other chapters of this book. It is worth noting that along with case studies and role plays, the use of these guides is very cost effective. In other words they cost only your time.

Assessment centres

To a certain extent I have already mentioned these. There are a number of purpose-built assessment centres around the country or, alternatively, there are consultants who can bring the 'centre' to you. This presupposes that your company has the necessary facilities and that you will not be testing for the type of skill displayed in outside activities. I have taken a number of assessment tools to companies to create an assessment centre which we can then run over a few days.

As I have already said, this list is not exhaustive and I am sure that there are other very fine ways of testing individual strengths and weaknesses. Of course all of the above do more than just test skills – they develop skills or in some cases identify the skills that need to be developed.

_____ 6 _____

The team accomplishes the task

By following the process outlined in steps one to five, there is a real chance for achievement. By monitoring each step, adjusting your approach if necessary, and certainly by giving and receiving feedback from the team, success will be that much easier to achieve. In looking at this very simple process we have identified some basic principles; if we adhere to these principles, then getting the job done right will become a way of life. Just as important as this, however, is the need to ensure that you have the right person doing the right job. When you do, you have a team not only efficient, but effective.

To summarise and to help you think in terms of your position at work, whatever that position may be, scan the following list and slot yourself into whichever step is applicable, and see the process through.

WHY PERFORMANCE MANAGEMENT? – SUMMARY

There are real benefits to all for successful performance management and for getting the right people in the right jobs. Ensure success by following these steps:

- Step 1 – Establish the vision, know your objectives

- Step 2 – Communicate the objectives to the management team

- Step 3 – Have them communicate the objectives to the team

- Step 4 – Invite the team to make suggestions accomplishing objectives

- Step 5 – Know individual strengths and assign appropriate tasks

- Step 6 – Monitor, feedback, adjusts and achieve

CHAPTER TWO

How to create a job purpose statement

In this chapter we examine:

■ How to avoid duplication of effort

■ How to create job purpose statements

■ How to write job descriptions

■ How to ensure you have an economy of effort

Having established a very simple process for getting the right people doing the right job, let us now look at a process for establishing why the job exists and what the main functions of the job are. Why the job exists can be explained in a short statement which is called a **job purpose statement**. What the main functions of the job are can be contained in a statement known as the **job description**. Notice that in writing these two statements we are answering two basic questions – *why* and *what*.

Job purpose statements

It is unlikely that you will get two job purpose statements exactly the same; if you do it probably means that you have created two or more jobs for the same purpose. This, of course, is not entirely wrong. It is to be expected that in large companies you will need several people working at the a same job. However, if the job has been created for the wrong reasons, then the problems you create outweigh any possible short-term benefits. The waste of time, duplication and frustration that this will create is sufficient, one would think, to ensure that it never happens. However, it does from time to time and the reasons can be many – here are just a few:

- Lack of clear objectives

- Lack of planning

- Panic (crisis management)

- Lack of trust

Let us look briefly at each of these reasons, if only to ensure that we understand the implications and the reasons why, and so avoid using them ourselves.

Lack of clear objectives

Since the objectives of the company have their roots in the mission statement, we are back to understanding why the company exists. If there are no clear objectives based on values and vision, the temptation is to operate a 'get rich quick' scenario, where business at any price is the motto. Under these circumstances jobs and people become expendable. The attitude is that you take on enough people to get a job or task accomplished, then you get rid of them. On the other hand, of course, you can have a company with vision and values and with objectives, but which has failed to communicate these downwards. You then have managers assuming objectives, which can lead to over-staffing. In both of these cases it would be rare to see job purpose statements produced or used. Why? Because job purpose statements are very closely linked to mission statements and why the company exists to do business. Clear objectives will ensure that job purpose statements are written and used, and will help avoid duplication of effort and an unnecessary waste of time and money.

Lack of planning

Have you ever driven along a road to see beside it several trucks with equipment, and what appears to be a multitude of workmen? Have you, on closer inspection, observed the hole being dug by two of the workmen while the rest stand by, watching? I have, and I have always thought that this has to be a terrible waste of resources and shows an incredible lack of planning. I have also witnessed departments in companies with dozens of people all doing the same job, but with at least half of them standing about or shifting paper. I have experienced the mass lay-off that redundancy brings and then have seen the company operate just as efficiently, meaner and leaner. Of course I am not advocating redundancy. This is a terrible waste of a company's greatest asset, provided, of course, that the lack of planning did not over-staff the company in the first place.

Panic (crisis management)

It is accepted that poor managers have the habit of surrounding themselves with people whom they hoard and keep in reserve for when the crises strike. Of course to them every day is a crisis, so the people stagnate and fail to develop, or they resign and go elsewhere. I have always been amazed at the excuses that crisis management creates to keep departments and sections over-staffed. They have this reservoir of reasons why they need big sections or big departments, and because, l suppose, it is natural to be cautious in business, it seems easy to sell the fear of what a crisis will do to deadlines in order to keep the personnel.

Lack of trust

This is perhaps the most insulting reason for having more than one person doing a job. Except for exceptional circumstances, i.e. training purposes, to have more than one person doing a job is not acceptable. To duplicate effort, to create the insecurity of one competing against the other, just to meet deadlines or 'cover your back', is really not on. It highlights some glaring deficiencies in a manager's skills and abilities when he/she has to resort to this tactic.

As I have said, there are a number of reasons why a job would be duplicated and these are just a few examples. Job purpose statements support the principle of having the right person doing the right job because they identify that the job is important and exists to enable the successful accomplishment of the company's objectives and mission statement. So, as managers we look at the range of jobs within our span of control, relate them to the mission statement and create a short statement which will say why the job exists. Let us have a look at a few golden rules regarding the writing of job purpose statements.

Job purpose statements – the golden rules

1 The statement should be short – one or two sentences will do.

2 The statement should say *why* the job exists.

3 The statement should be specific to the job being described.

4 The statement must tie in with the mission statement.

Remember, we are not looking for a list of tasks; we are looking for a short statement explaining why the job exists. If you have trouble you might ask yourself, what would be the effect if the job did not exist? Here is an example which might prove helpful:

> 'To develop the sales of XYZ Company products and services, by recruiting and developing quality support managers and salespersons within agreed objectives.'

This is the job purpose statement for a manager in a branch office of a large sales company. Notice that it avoids listing tasks and broadly gives the reason why the job exists. To be totally helpful you would need to see this company's mission statement, but since we are not trying to justify the statement, but just using it as an example, we'll leave it at this.

Let us now look at the benefits of having such a statement, both for the individual and the company, and see the wide-ranging spin-offs that come from such a simple thing.

1 The job holder has a very clear picture of why he/she is employed.

2 The job holder can see what results are expected (at least in a general sense).

3 The job holder can identify easily how he/she will be assessed.

4 The parameters for authority and accountability are clear.

5 The 'big picture', i.e. the mission statement, identifies the value of this job

6 The statements assist in putting the right person in the right job.

7 Enthusiasm and morale are very high.

8 Career development planning is made easier.

9 Personal development can be more precise.

10 There is greater efficiency and *effectiveness* throughout the organisation.

Job descriptions

I have mentioned job descriptions, but these almost become redundant once you have a good job purpose statement. All the job description does is to identify the *what* of the job, the tasks that might make up the day-to-day activities.

Of course, if you are new to the job, having a list of tasks can be very helpful; after all it is hard enough trying to discover how the company wants a job done, without wondering precisely what it is you are supposed to be doing. But once you are experienced, the strength of having a broad statement that tells you why your job exists and then being given the freedom to decide for yourself what you will do and how you will do it, makes for a very dynamic company.

The importance of knowing what to do

Many years ago, when I left one industry to join another, I experienced first hand what it was like to know why I was employed and yet not know what I should be doing. I had joined the financial services industry as a salesperson and had completed two weeks of intensive training on products and the sales process. I was employed on a self-employed contract that paid commission only. This simply meant that if I did not sell I did not get paid. However, following these two weeks of training and on a Monday morning in April, I took a sun-bed out into my garden and lay in the early spring sunshine sunbathing. My wife, who was going about her chores of washing and cleaning, came out into the garden to hang out some washing. She observed me and then quietly asked, 'Brian, why aren't you working?' The question took me by surprise and for a moment I was tongue tied. Then I honestly replied, 'Well, I am not sure what I'm supposed to be doing'. With her usual insight and forthrightness, she said, 'Don't you think you had better find out, otherwise we are not going to eat next month'. So of course I did find out. I discovered all the many activities and tasks that I would need to do in order to be a successful salesman.

I have found that this scenario presents itself whenever a new job is obtained or a new person has come to work for me, and it is very helpful to give a job description that outlines the tasks and activities that will make up the functions of the job. I have found that with senior managers and executives, just having a job purpose statement has been sufficient for them to decide what should be done and how to do it.

The process for writing job descriptions is as follows:

1 Know the purpose of the job.

2 List the main tasks associated with the job.

3 Recognise that there may be other tasks or functions occasionally performed.

4 Identify the parameters of the job's authority.

5 State accountability – to whom and for what.

6 Identify the skills necessary for the job and the standards at which they are to be performed. (*See* Chapter 3)

7 Include the remuneration package.

8 Include the conditions of working.

Remember that all of the above is what the person doing the job will do and get. To a certain extent the standards will influence *how* it will be done, as well as lay down company procedures and the company culture. Job descriptions aid the quest to get the right person doing the right job. They will at times become a selection tool for the would-be employee.

Job descriptions – a selection tool?

I remember interviewing a candidate for a job that I had been advertising. The advertisement, out of necessity, only listed generalities in terms of what the job was. It attracted a large response and, unfortunately, most of the candidates were unsuitable. However, several of the candidates were clearly suitable and well qualified. This particular candidate fell into the latter category, and I was optimistic about him coming to work with me. I was impressed when he asked me for a job description, and he was suitably impressed when I gave him one, but it took only a moment for him to decide that it was not for him. Some of the tasks listed were clearly not to his liking and he determined that it was something he did not want to do. As disappointed as I was, I was very grateful that I found this out before he took the job. It would have been a very expensive mistake on my part to have found out later.

On another occasion and in very similar circumstances, I was able to use the job description as a selection tool. This time the candidate was anxious to join me. He had interviewed well although I was having some reservations. I showed the job description to him and watched his face as he read through it; I noticed once or twice that he grimaced and I probed to find out why. He did his best to hide his concerns, but I had observed him and I knew that it would be wrong to pursue the career opportunity with him.

Accountability

I mentioned accountability in the process for writing job descriptions and it would be worth pointing out the benefits that come from having people who clearly know the extent of their accountability and to whom they account working with you. When something goes wrong, and we all know that from time to time it does, the last thing I want to hear is, 'It wasn't my responsibility' or 'Don't blame me, it wasn't my fault'. If I have to apportion blame at all, it would be very helpful to know just whose responsibility it was. Better still, because of the job purpose statement and the job description, I want to hear people accept responsibility, tell me how the situation can be retrieved, and make a commitment not to repeat the mistake. I have to say that my experience has taught me that the latter scenario can and often does become the norm. The enormous strengths that come out of this are, of course, that time is spent on putting things right rather than trying to find out whose fault it was. Job purpose statements and job descriptions are of immense importance in using criteria-based interviewing and appraisals. They begin to establish very firmly that we know what the job is and that we can begin to match people against very precise known skills and qualities. The benefits are enormous both to the individual and the organisation. Gone will be the days when someone is given a job just because there is a job to give. Gone will be the days when management will discover too late that the right person is not in the right job.

To summarise this important chapter and its content, let me list the benefits of writing job purpose statements and job descriptions in a broader sense than that which I have already done.

HOW TO CREATE A JOB PURPOSE STATEMENT – SUMMARY

- Job purpose statements say why the job exists

- Job descriptions identify the tasks and activities that make up the job

- Both statements have their roots in the mission statement of the company

- Both are critical to criteria-based interviewing

- Appraisal and assessment is made more objective

- Individuals know the broad parameters of appraisal/assessment

- Individuals accept responsibility and accountability

- There is greater efficiency and effectiveness throughout the organisation

- We get the right people doing the right job

CHAPTER THREE

Identifying the skills for the job

In this chapter we examine:

- The importance of mission statements

- What are competences?

- How to set the competences (skills) for each job

- How to test the competences

- What are the benchmarks or ancor points?

- How to create interview guides

- How to conduct criteria-based interviews

- How to create job profiles

In this chapter we are going to look at the importance of identifying the skills that go with the job. We will look at the process for agreeing competences for the company, and how to go about deciding which of all the competences identified are the ones that are key to the achievement of the objectives outlined in the job purpose statement. These are important because they will form the basis for the quarterly or annual appraisal, and we do not want to be appraising competences that are not necessary to improve the performance of the job holder.

If the company has not set the competences for each job, all is not totally lost. As a manager you can decide, along with the job holder, the competences needed for the job, and you can even start to set anchor points for the job (these are described later in the chapter).

I know only too well the frustration that a manager feels when, having learned a principle, he/she then discovers that company practices make it difficult or even impossible to implement that principle. But I have also discovered that all over the world, in small and large companies, good managers apply principles at whatever level they are at and get good results, even though with company backing the results could be even greater. So do not be deterred. It may well be your branch, section or department that shows the way forward and sets the example that will lead the boss to notice the difference and ask 'What are you doing that is creating this success?'

This chapter is written to help you implement criteria-based appraisals in your organisation. It is a simple, step-by-step guide and the power of this process lies in the fact that the steps are exactly the same whether it is a large or small company, or a section, branch or department of a company.

Criteria = competences or skills

When I was a boy I used to watch my grandfather make cricket bats. He was one of the old school, brought up to believe that if a job was worth doing it was worth doing well, and he was a craftsman. Not only did he learn his craft, he practised his craft and for him there were no short cuts. I watched him for hours as first he would choose his timber: he would fell the tree, cut it into rounds, then clefts, then stack the clefts to let them dry. He knew every grain, every potential weakness – he knew at a glance the quality of the wood he was to work with. When he started his work, it was to be all hand work, no machinery. He would shape and shave the wood by hand and finally produce a cricket bat suitable for an England player – often that was where the bat was destined to go. I used to wonder at his skill, how lovingly he handled the material that was to become the finished product. Not only was his skill in knowing his material and his craft, but also he could do every part of the job – his skill with handtools was something to be marvelled at.

Too often, I believe, we think of skills in connection with trades and crafts, probably because they are very visible. I mean you can see when someone is cutting something badly with a saw. When it comes to 'people skills' I do not believe that skills are so readily seen, and for this reason so often a 'job well done' is measured by the outputs, not the skills that go into getting the result. How often have you seen a department or section, or indeed a branch office, succeed in spite of the manager, not because of him, yet because the results are good, he is judged to be a good manager. If we can identify the *inputs*, the skills that are needed to do the job well, we can start to look for those skills in the person who is to do the job. We can positively identify what it is that will bring about the *outputs,* i.e. the results, and match individual skills with those required.

This is what criteria-based interviewing is all about and there is a very clear process to follow, both in carrying out such an interview and in making sure that the company structure complements what a criteria-based interview will produce. When we use the term *criteria,* think of skills because the skills of a job become the criteria when we use this interviewing technique. In other words, I could call this technique, skills-based interviewing. It would be the same thing because it is the skills of the job that I would first identify, then attempt to match these with the skills of the person being interviewed for that job. Let us first look at the process for creating the right environment in which criteria-based interviewing thrives (see Figure 2).

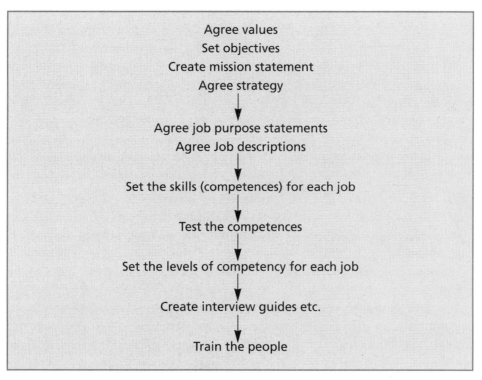

Agree values
Set objectives
Create mission statement
Agree strategy

Agree job purpose statements
Agree Job descriptions

Set the skills (competences) for each job

Test the competences

Set the levels of competency for each job

Create interview guides etc.

Train the people

Figure 2

What we will now do is work through this process, getting each step clear in the mind; then we will return to look at the interviewing technique more precisely in terms of process.

Values, objectives, mission statements, strategy

Although much has already been said about these crucial steps in Chapter 1, they are so important there is justification in making further comment. To give an analogy, try to imagine a set of drawings, let us make them drawings of a house. The layout of the plot, the details of the foundations, the plans for each room, the roof construction, the plumbing layout and the electrical circuits are all contained on different drawing sheets, as are all the other detailed drawings that are needed to construct the house as it has been visualised. Can you imagine the chaos if each of the tradesmen responsible for the various trades were given only the drawing with their specifications outlined? It is the practice in house building to have a full set of drawings available for all to see, so that everyone gets the 'big picture', everyone can see the finished article, and can clearly see where their individual contribution fits into the whole building programme.

So it is with mission statements; they become the *big picture*, they are the hook upon which all else hangs. When difficulties arise and it is hard to see the way forward, mission statements clarify, enlarge and give a sense of direction and purpose. The overall strategy and the objectives which are like milestones that allow a company to measure its progress towards the vision, wrapped up in the values of the company, all expressed in a short but powerful statement, give the employees as well as management a real sense of direction and purpose.

Job purpose statements, job descriptions

Again, the whole of Chapter 2 dealt with the importance of these two steps in the process. It is vital, however, that you do not miss out these steps. Knowing what you want from a job helps to identify the person you want to do the job, both in terms of academic qualifications and the other skills which qualify an individual to give you what you want. In addition, of course, these two statements will have their roots in the mission statement and will show how the job, when done correctly, contributes to the overall objectives of the company

Set the skills (competences) for each job

You may think that in almost every case this has been done, for instance clerks, secretaries, supervisors etc., have been hired for many years and there is a clear picture of what is expected of them in the job. While it is true that the *hard competences* are obvious, it is not always so with the *soft competences*, and if you remember we discussed the differences between the two in chapter 1. Soft competences are the interpersonal skills etc. Academic qualifications will have been set perhaps a long time ago, so these skills will be known and will not have to be set again, unless of course the job has changed. In a changing world jobs are changing all the time. The changes are sometimes so subtle that often we can have the situation where unqualified people are doing a job they were once qualified for. So, what do we do? Let us assume that we are starting from scratch, that we are creating a company with all its various jobs to fill, and that we haven't actually created a picture of effective performance in that job, so we are unclear of the skills needed to do the job. In starting from scratch so to speak, we will see that the principles we are about to use can be applied to whatever stage you are at, and at worst can serve as a back-to-basics analysis.

It is a fact that many jobs will require some of the same skills, in other words it is unlikely that each job would have a list of very separate and unique skills, although some may. Therefore it is reasonable to assume that from a list of say some 50 to 60 skills (competences), each job would draw its own list of say 12 to 15, and in many instances they would be similar, perhaps with only one or two truly unique to that particular job. Remember, we are now talking across the whole organisation, so we start the process by getting this list of 50 to 60 competences.

It would be well to point out that from now on I shall refer to skills as competences. If you have difficulty with the word competence, try to substitute the word skill, but it is important that we use the terminology that is widely used in industry.

The following is a typical list of competences from which a smaller number can be identified as necessary for any particular job:

- Adaptability
- Attention to detail
- Commitment
- Communication
- Compliance
- Creativity
- Listening
- Monitoring
- Motivation
- Negotiation
- Persuasiveness
- Planning

- Decisiveness
- Delegation
- Development of others
- Energy
- Impact
- Independence
- Initiative
- Innovativeness
- Integrity
- Judgement

- Leadership
- Presentation
- Problem analysis
- Problem-solving
- Resilience
- Sensitivity
- Team-building
- Tenacity
- Tolerance
- Vision

Now of course this is not an exhaustive list, just an example of the competences that go with jobs. The difficulty comes in knowing which competence goes with which job, recognising of course that many of these competences are desirable whatever the job, and indeed may be essential for any number of jobs.

Keeping in mind that we are moving rapidly towards using these competences in an appraisal situation, it does become very important that the competence is in fact needed to do the job well and that the person holding the job not only recognises this, but agrees.

So, we have a picture of what the job is to produce, we know why it exists. We know that certain academic qualifications are necessary and we know that some competences are essential and others desirable, if the job is to be done efficiently and effectively. From our list we can take an educated guess as to which of the competencies are essential. We could draw on personal experience, especially if we have done a particular job, or we can draw on the experience of other organisations. Whichever way we use, we should set the competencies for the job, because now we are going to test them, to make sure that we have got it right, and to make sure that the job holder agrees. Of course once competences have been set and agreed, it is not necessary to test them again or get agreement from each new job holder as to their validity. This only happens if the job changes dramatically.

Test the competences

The testing of competences is a relatively simple process but it requires great skill, especially in the art of interviewing. Because we will look at the technique in detail later in this chapter, we will deal only with the process here.

_____ 1 _____
Say what the competences are for each job

The first step in the process is to publish the competences that go with the job, making sure that accompanying each competence is a definition statement. This is a short but succint statement defining exactly what the competence is. For example:

> **DECISION-MAKING**
> Making timely decisions in line with objectives by collating information and prioritising information to judge the correct course of action.

With a short statement such as the one above accompanying each competence, all who read it can get a common understanding not only of what the competence is, but also how to use it. Of course it is important to test the understanding of the definition. To do this it is simply a matter of question and discussion, or perhaps giving another example if necessary. Once the definition is understood and accepted you can then move to step 2 in the process.

_____ 2 _____
Obtain the evidence that supports the need for the competence

This requires that we get evidence to support that the competence is necessary or desirable. We want to find out how often the competence is used, in what context and to what effect. We can even find out whether it should be used but is not, either because of a development need or because of the system, a peer or a boss being obstructive. We get the evidence by asking for examples of when the competence was used, and it is important that we get more than one example. If you cannot get more than one example, the questions you need to be asking are:

- How important is this competence?
- What is the effect of it not being used very often?
- Why isn't it being used very often?
- What would be the effect if it were used often?

The difficulty comes because plenty of evidence and a lack of evidence can both support the necessity and the desirability of a competence.

In the testing process it is worth noting that not every job holder of the same job needs to be interviewed. For example if I were running a sales company with 100 sales managers, interviewing 30 per cent of the managers would give me the same result as interviewing all 100. In other words, 30 managers interviewed will validate the competence as well as 100 managers interviewed.

When testing competences, there is great value in asking those being interviewed whether or not there are competences they use which have not been identified. Likewise, if we were testing 12 to 15 competences, it would be of value to send out a list of 25 or so and let the interviewees' choose their own 12 to 15 by prioritising them. The benefits that come from doing this are many and have their roots in the fact that the people doing the job know the job best. They are also doing the job a in a constant environment of change so will know which competence has become less important and which competences now are more valuable. Of course they will also know if there are competences needed now that have not been included for appraisal.

Using the scenario that we started with, i.e. a start-up situation, I have assumed that we have recruited people who have done the job for another organisation.

Once the competences have been published, tested and accepted, these are the yardsticks by which performance will be measured; they will be the performance criteria that will identify whether the job is being well done or not. They will be the criteria for recommending promotion or further training and development.

Set the levels of competence for each job

I have already mentioned that a competence may be desirable in any number of jobs, as well as necessary. For example, if supervisors are expected to be decisive, so are managers and so are executives, yet it would be foolish to expect them to perform at the same level. So now having set and tested the competences, we can set the anchor points or benchmarks for each job. This means that while any number of jobs might have the same competence, it is expected that there might be different levels for each job. The anchor point or benchmark is the level of performance expected for the job being done.

There are a number of ways of doing this, and a number of different levels that can be set. My experience is with a 1–7 set of levels. Each level has a descriptive statement which identifies a level of performance. For example, suppose we use the competence **sourcing** (and I am taking this competence from the job of sales manager in the financial services industry), the levels might look like this:

SOURCING

The ability to provide a constant stream of high-quality recruits (this is the definition). The job requires the ability to:

7 Identify high quality individuals from all walks of life and professions, knowing how to approach these individuals, having an approach script, and having a steady stream of new recruits throughout the year.

5 Be sociably mobile, having access to a number of sources from which possible recruits may come and maintaining a high activity in recruiting interviews.

3 Attract others to look at career opportunities through advertising, job centres and other passive recruiting centres.

1 Approach various recruiting centres to sell the career opportunity.

You will note that although seven levels of competence can be reached, only four are given descriptive statements. This is because if someone is performing better than level 3 but not quite up to level 5, it is assumed that they are performing at level 4, and so on. What can now be done, having these levels so clearly identified, is to set the level at which the job holder should be performing – the anchor point or benchmark. Once this is done, everyone doing the job can be appraised against the anchor point, and in so doing identify development needs, promotion, bonuses and the value that the individual creates for the company.

It is also possible to profile the job as well, so that future employees can be measured against a known job profile (see example later in the chapter).

Create interview guides

Once you have set, tested and anchor pointed the competences, you can now design an interview guide to help you when selecting candidates for the jobs you have vacant. There follows an example of such a guide. It will not be complete in that every competence will not be shown, but it will illustrate just two to give you an example. Again, because my experience is in the financial services industry, it will relate to that industry; however the principles can be used in any industry and it would be a simple matter to create an interview guide for any job in any industry where the competences have been set, tested and anchored.

Just to briefly describe the following pages, first there is an explanation of what criteria-based interviews are (remember I pointed out that the competences are the criteria). The next page gives the job purpose statement, in this case it is for a Branch Manager in a sales office. The next page lists the competences for a Branch Manager (these are actual competences set and tested by a client company that I worked with). Then comes a self-assessment test, which is completed by the candidate and serves the purpose of getting a self-evaluation first. All of these competences and the evaluation the candidate makes will later be tested and the interviewer can make comparisons between what the candidate thinks and reality. Then comes each competence, its definition, and a number of questions designed to get evidence from the candidate as to the extent to which the competence has been understood and used in the working environment. Let us go this far.

CONDUCTING CRITERIA-BASED INTERVIEWS

The following pages contain the competences that have been set and tested for the job of Branch Manager in a direct sales force. While it is not expected that each candidate will be strong in the use of every competence, there needs to be some indication that the candidate has a basic understanding of each competence and has reached a level of performance in each.

To help you to determine what that level is, there are a number of questions that should be asked and some examples are given. Please note that these are not all the questions that should be asked but are an example of the type of question you should be asking. You will notice that these are open-ended questions that seek for evidence and clarification. They may appear to be very challenging questions, but that is exactly what they are intended to do – to find out what has been done through actual experiences.

When you get the answers to these questions, you are then asked to make an evaluation. This evaluation is a judgement as to which level of competence you feel the candidate has performed, and you will note that there are five levels. The reason the rating goes only to level 5 is because it is unlikely that the anchor points for any job will be set at level 7, and it is against the anchor point that you will want to evaluate the performance of the candidate.

The candidate will have already self-assessed himself/herself in some of the competences, so you will be able to compare your rating with that of the candidate. To justify your rating you will have had to take copious notes, recording the evidence of performance as you have uncovered it. These notes should be clear and precise so that anyone reading them can see why you have rated the candidate as you have.

BRANCH MANAGER (DIRECT SALES)

JOB PURPOSE STATEMENT:

To develop the sales of XYZ Company products and services by recruiting and developing quality support management and salespersons within agreed objectives.

THE XYZ COMPANY COMPETENCES FOR BRANCH MANAGERS

Motivating others

Development of others

Commitment to achieving results

Influencing morale

Team-building

Planning

Decision-making

Communication/feedback

Empathy and understanding

Quality and efficiency

Monitoring progress

Counselling

Adaptability

Time management

Initiative

SELF-ASSESSMENT
(to be completed by the candidate)

Check the response that best describes your use of the following competences.

5 = excellent   1 = poor

	5	4	3	2	1
PLANNING – Establishing a course of action for self and/or others to accomplish a specific goal; planning proper assignments of personnel and appropriate allocation of resources.	☐	☐	☐	☐	☐
DECISION-MAKING – Making timely decisions in line with objectives by collating information, prioritising information to judge the correct course of action.	☐	☐	☐	☐	☐
COMMUNICATION/FEEDBACK – Communicating facts and concepts effectively both in writing and orally, then giving positive and negative feedback on performance/behaviour in an acceptable way.	☐	☐	☐	☐	☐
MOTIVATING OTHERS – Applying of appropriate interpersonal and motivational styles and methods in guiding individuals or groups towards task accomplishment and the achievement of business goals.	☐	☐	☐	☐	☐
DEVELOPMENT OF OTHERS – Developing the skills and competences of others through training and development activities related to current and future jobs.	☐	☐	☐	☐	☐
COMMITMENT TO ACHIEVING RESULTS – Showing commitment to the achievement of results and targets by accepting responsibility, owning the task, and applying effective application of effort and resources, combined with passion, belief and energy.	☐	☐	☐	☐	☐
RESILIENCE – Maintaining consistency of performance under pressure and/or opposition.	☐	☐	☐	☐	☐

TESTING COMPETENCES

Planning and monitoring progress

Establishing a course of action for self and/or others to accomplish a specific goal; planning proper assignment of personnel and appropriate allocation of resources; monitoring progress on tasks and activities by using system control and checking against the original plan; giving feedback and redirecting efforts if necessary.

Questions to ask

What steps do you take to organise your work?
How could you improve?
How did you set your performance goals for the year?
How did you coordinate them?
How did you prioritise them?
Tell me about a typical week.
Thinking of your last meeting, how did you ensure that it would
    be successful?
How did you involve others?
What problems did you face and how did you deal with them?
How do you determine the progress you have made towards your goals?
Which activities do you monitor on a regular basis?
How do you monitor them?
What are the ratios that you feel are important and why?
Tell me about the time you tracked the progress of someone else.
    What problems did you have to overcome?

Decision-making

Making timely decisions in line with objectives by collating information, prioritising information to judge the correct course of action.

Questions to ask

What was the last major decision you made?
How did you go about making it?
Which decisions do you find easy to make?
What decision did you make that was wrong?
What did you do about it?
How important is it to make quick decisions? Why?
What do you need to know in order to make a decision?
How do you feel about changing a decision?
How would you go about it?

▶

Why would you change a decision?
When would you consult others before making a decision?
Under what circumstances would you not make a decision?
How do you feel about people who do not make quick decisions? Why?
How do you deal with decisions that are going to be unpopular?
How do you deliver unpopular decisions?
How do you get unpopular decisions accepted?
What are the overriding factors in major-decision making?

This interruption of the interview guide is to allow me to give some advice and some clarification as to the process we are following. First, although I have shown only two examples of the competences with their definitions and some recommended questions to ask, please remember that each of the 12 to 15 competences that are associated with the job will need to be tested. This means an interview time of around two to three hours and will also mean that the interviewer will need to take copious notes of all the answers given. It is possible to include notepaper in the interview guide itself so that it becomes a record of what took place, or separate sheets of notepaper can be attached to the guide. The important thing to remember is that people do not remember, and if you carry out criteria-based interviews and do not take notes, your evaluation will become subjective because feelings and a few short memories will be all the evidence you can present. Also worth remembering is the benefit of having others read your notes, making their own evaluation, comparing it with yours and then supporting the overall evaluation because there was sufficient evidence upon which they could base a judgement.

Once all the competences have been tested, in other words once you have asked numerous open questions and got some real evidence (or not as the case may be), you can then make your evaluation. In doing this you will be able to create a personal profile for each candidate. This profile will be made up of your assessment of where they rate in terms of understanding and using the competences in the work environment. A job profile will have already been created because the anchor points or benchmarks will have been set for each job, and a very visible graph will be available against which you can match the profile of the individual.

It is important to realise that it is unlikely that a perfect match will occur each time you compare individual profiles with the job profile. This is because, hopefully, the individual will be performing above the level of the benchmark, or in some instances below the benchmark. The benefit of making comparisons is that you can decide whether under performance is such that it renders the candidate unsuitable for the job, or over performance the candidate is capable of a bigger job, or that with some development training the candidate will be fine for the job.

The following two pages are examples of what a job profile might look like for a Branch Manager in a sales company, and a personal profile of an applicant for that job (both are fictitious).

JOB PROFILE – BRANCH MANAGER

INTERPERSONAL SKILLS	5	4	3	2	1
Counselling			*		
Communication & feedback		*			
Empathy & understanding			*		
LEADERSHIP					
Motivating others		*			
Influencing morale		*			
Initiative			*		
Decision-making		*			
Developing others	*				
Commitment to achieve results	*				
Team-building		*			
MANAGING RESOURCES					
Planning			*		
Monitoring progress			*		
Quality & efficiency		*			
Time management		*			

CANDIDATE PROFILE

INTERPERSONAL SKILLS	5	4	3	2	1
Counselling					
Communication & feedback					
Empathy & understanding					
LEADERSHIP					
Motivating others					
Influencing morale					
Initiative					
Decision-making					
Developing others					
Commitment to achieve results					
Team-building					
MANAGING RESOURCES					
Planning					
Monitoring progress					
Quality & effciency					
Time management					

These are not the only tools of assessment you might use in an interview guide. You may want to include some numerical pointer on such things as appearance, punctuality, ambition, body language, performance under pressure, etc. However, it is not the intent here to present a complete interview guide, merely to demonstrate the content as far as competences are concerned, and how valuable the evidence becomes when you start to make important decisions about employment.

Train the people

This is the last step in the flow chart presented in Fig. 2 on page 29. Having a clear picture of what criteria-based interviewing will do, now you must train those who will use it, and it is not easy. The interviewing technique alone takes some getting used to and is full of pitfalls. My recommendation is to obtain training for your trainers and then run a continuous training programme for all those who use this process or who will use it. There are a number of good training programmes to be had in the market place, as well as some useful video films.

Let us now look at the process involved in the actual interview, together with some of the pitfalls and habits to be avoided. This in itself will start the training programme.

Criteria-based intervewing technique

Let us start by looking at some general interview guidelines; we might call them some golden rules.

The golden rules for conducting interviews

1 Ask a range of questions such as:
- Broad open-ended questions (*What* makes for effective performance?)
- Focused open-ended questions (*Why* is that important?)
- Probing questions (*How* would I see that?)
- Reflective questions (So X is important because of Y …)

2 Always get concrete examples, i.e. what was actually done, not what someone thinks should be done.

3 Qualify broad statements, i.e. 'he produced a quality piece of work' – what does this mean?

4 Try to get comparisons between the examples you get from the interviewee and their peers.

5 Tackle the same issue from different angles.

6 Write down what is said – copious notes.

7 Continually check understanding by summarising.

Now let us look at each of these seven **golden rules** more closely to ensure that there is no misunderstanding as to what is meant.

Ask a range of questions

During an interview there will be lots of questions that will bring hard facts as answers, such as places worked and for how long. Usually these answers will emerge quite naturally as you follow a guide or even complete application forms. It is the wider information that we are seeking when we use open-ended questions – information that explains and clarifies, reveals feelings and attitudes and tests knowledge and skill. Broad open-ended questions are questions that call for opinions based on experience or knowledge. They reveal the depth of understanding and application that the interviewee has regarding a particular process, procedure or practice. That is why, in the example used in number 1, the question asks, '*What* makes for effective performance?'. The interviewee has probably mentioned effective performance and now the interviewer wants to know what is effective performance in the opinion and experience of the interviewee.

The same explanation fits the other open-ended questions illustrated in number 1. Focused open-ended questions call for the interviewee to justify a statement or belief. They test understanding, but more importantly they test to see whether the interviewee has an opinion and whether that opinion carries some conviction and belief: *Why* do you feel this way? *Why* is this important? *Why* did you do this in this way? and so on.

Probing questions call for clarification and explanation. They are used to enable the interviewer to get a more complete answer and to avoid misunderstanding. For example, during an interview the interviewee makes an important throw away statement like, '*I used to do things differently to get better effect*'. The probing questions that would follow such a statement might be: What did you do differently? How would I have seen the difference? If I were observing, how would I see you being more effective? and so on.

Reflective questions allow the interviewee to think over what has been said and to evaluate whether the information is accurate and complete. They also ensure that there has been no misunderstanding. For example, suppose that during the interview the interviewee says, *'My performance would have been better if I had received better management'*. The reflective question that would follow such a remark might be, *'So you are saying that your manager prevented you from being more productive, is that right?'*.

2. Get concrete examples

You will find that when you ask for examples there is a tendency for people to waffle. Why? Because it is easy to say how things ought to be or ought to be done, and it is easy to remember how we feel about something and to imagine that the circumstances and people fit the way we feel. Often we can fall into the trap of allowing one small negative experience to convince us that that is the way it always was or is. By asking for solid examples to substantiate statements, we start to find out how real the opinion or performance of the interviewee really is. For example, our interviewee says something like, *'I was very good at keeping the peace'*, to which we would reply, *'Give me an example of the last time you kept the peace'*. Then we would use probing questions to test the reply, use reflective questions to ensure that we understood and to challenge statements, open questions to get a fuller picture and reveal belief, attitude and feelings, and then possibly ask for another example. The more solid the example, the more valid the statement, and the more valid the performance.

3. Qualify broad statements

Often the most difficult to do, this step is very important. I remember interviewing a candidate who was immaculately dressed, presented himself well, answered questions positively and was enjoying the interview very much, until I challenged him on his performance data. I had probed to find out the level of his performance and he had confidently told me that he was always in the top ten salesmen in the branch in which he worked. This was intended to impress me, and I might have fallen into the trap because most companies publish only the top ten or so. But I was prompted to ask, 'How many salesmen work out of your office?'. It transpired that there were only ten. I then asked for levels of business and broke this down to precise activity. I was able to compare this performance with the performance of the people working out of my office and it was not impressive. Qualifying broad statements will allow you to make comparisons and therefore get accurate pictures of what a candidate has to offer.

4. Get comparisons

I have already dealt with this in the preceding paragraph in the sense that comparisons can be made when you qualify statements, and it is useful to try to get a picture of what a performance displayed elsewhere will look like in your own environment. Of equal value of course are comparisons between peers, to try to see how equals are performing and to test whether all are being subjected to the same difficulties. Part of the people problem-solving process is to make comparisons to see how many other people might be experiencing the same set of problems. This step is exactly the same principle. By making comparisons we can find out what is an isolated set of circumstances and what is more generally being experienced. Then we can evaluate individual ability to deal with those circumstances.

5. Tackle from different angles

The same as asking the same question in a different way, the intention is to test validity and to ensure understanding and sometimes to get an answer. For example, suppose that during the interviewing process, while trying to establish the strengths and weaknesses of the candidate and in response to the question regarding weaknesses, the candidate could not identify any. Try as you might, using silences and repeating the question, still no weaknesses were identified. Then you might ask, coming from a different angle, 'If I asked your husband/wife what are your weaknesses, what would he/she say?' I have used this approach on numerous occasions using husband/wife, previous manager, work colleagues and friends to allow an individual to admit to weaknesses and to identify them.

Don't be afraid to come back to an issue. There is nothing wrong in repeating questions at a later stage in a different manner to expand on answers that you felt were unsatisfactory or needing clarification. Another good practice is to get another opinion. I used my secretary a lot in the interviewing process, not in a formal way but informally. Of course I valued her judgement and I always kept her remarks in perspective, and often she was able to give me a different angle on a candidate, allowing me to see from a new perspective.

6. Take copious notes

There is an opinion that taking notes detract from an interview, not allowing for constant eye contact and showing an interest. I do not subscribe to this opinion even though some of the argument is valid. I believe that the benefit of taking good notes more than compensates for the momentary loss of eye contact. What you get, which is of enormous value, is lots of evidence – recorded evidence – notes than can be evaluated later when the memory dims and when the emotion of personal contact is just a memory. These notes can be evaluated by friends and colleagues, they can be used to prompt further questions by yourself, and they become an important part of a candidate file. I made it a habit to take copious notes and to keep them on file and many times I was able to use them to qualify my opinions when discussing a candidate with the boss or a colleague. Of equal value, they often showed me areas of concern that I had not probed and further questions that I needed to ask in order to make informed decisions. Being a good interviewer in terms of style and manner is one thing. Add to this great strength the ability to accumulate and analyse information and data through taking good notes, and you have the making of an excellent interviewer, one who makes few mistakes.

The common errors when conducting interviews

As well as the golden rules of dos, there are three rules that cover the common errors that occur when conducting criteria-based interviews. These are:

1. Failure to focus on a real event or a real person

This is probably the biggest fault and error when conducting these interviews. It is so easy to allow the person being interviewed to slip into giving generalities, to say what they think should happen, or what they would do, rather than what they did. The interview being lengthy actually encourages the interviewer to grasp at any response that seems to be evidence, and if you are not careful the only evidence you get is prescriptive, i.e. what should happen. What we are *not* looking for in the first instance is an opinion. What we want is an *actual event* with *real people* so that we can make an evaluation as to how well the competence *was used*. I can tell you from experience that of all the errors, this is the one that needs to be avoided. This is the one that will present itself the most.

2. The information given is too general

For some reason people tend not to give too much detail. It is almost as if they think you were there and can fill in the gaps yourself. Press for detail. Ask questions to help you understand, especially concerning the scenario in which the example is being given. Try to imagine that you know nothing and so you have to find out everything, assuming nothing.

3. Not being persistent

When you start to press people for precise examples there will be embarrassing silences, especially when you ask for more than one example. Most of us can give one example readily, perhaps two, but start to probe for three, then four, and the grey cells are working overtime, unless, of course, the competence is used on a regular basis, and that is what we are trying to find out. Competences as skills are like any other skill, they are only strengths if used regularly, and the more regularly they are used the higher the level will become at which they can be used. So, do not be put off by silences, no matter how embarrassing it may become. Wait, and give people the time to collect their thoughts, then probe for more evidence. Use phrases like, 'Tell me some more examples', or 'Does any other instance spring to mind?', or 'What else can you tell me?'. While a lack of evidence in any competence does not mean that the individual cannot use the skill, it does suggest that if the job you want them to do requires that the competence is used a lot, there may be some development need.

Preparing for interviews

Now that we have identified some dos and don'ts, let us look at the actual interview and just recount some of the things that we will need by way of preparation. Remember that the interview will take approximately two to three hours.

First, you should have available an interview guide book. This will contain instructions and a list of the competences, their definitions and some sample questions to ask. It will also contain the profile of the job in terms of the anchor points for each competence. It would be helpful if you had the statements for each level of competence, i.e. 7–5–3–1, for each competence so that you have some idea at which level you are making comparisons. Then, of course, you will need to make sure that you have plenty of notepaper and pencils/pens.

Secondly, and this is true for all interviews, you should make sure that you will be uninterrupted. You should also choose a suitable office or interview room, one that will not be too stuffy or too cold – two hours is a long interview.

Thirdly, after suitable introductions and setting the candidate at ease, you should explain what it is that you are going to do. Of equal importance is to say why. Remember we are trying to get the right people in the right job – this has to be in everyone's interest. Explain that you will take notes and that you will ask a lot of searching questions. It is important that you do this in a non-threatening way, more by way of explaining the process.

Fourthly, follow the interview guide and get the self-assessment done early. You will need this to make some comparisons between what the candidate thinks and the real situation. In saying this I do not wish to imply that people are dishonest, but perceptions rarely meet reality, and at the end of the interview it is the evidence that the candidate has given that will allow you to compare real experience with what the candidate believes are his/her strengths.

This technique is not something that is mastered overnight. It takes practice and to those who practise the most the skill will come more readily. You will find that the technique becomes a habit and that you use it in every interview scenario. Whether you are interviewing your children, your wife/husband, or at work, criteria-based interviewing is a powerful tool for getting the truth.

IDENTIFYING THE SKILLS FOR THE JOB – SUMMARY

- Mission statements and job purpose statements determine the job you want done

- Each job will have around 12 to 15 competences that are needed

- Having identified them, produce a short definition statement

- Test these competences by interviewing approximately 30 per cent of those doing the job

- Set the anchor points (short descriptions of levels of performance) for each job

- Create a job profile

- Create interview guides so that individuals can be matched against the job

- Train your managers in the use of criteria-based interviewing techniques

---

CHAPTER FOUR

Setting objectives

In this chapter we examine:

- How to set objectives

- Identifying key objectives

- Measuring objectives

- Identifying competences associated with objectives

- How to ensure everyone pulls in the same direction

I don't suppose there is anyone in the western world, who is an adult, who hasn't heard of, or been involved in, the making of New Year Resolutions. These are no more than yearly objectives, something that we want to accomplish, and they are usually associated with quality of life. By this I mean making life more pleasant, more enjoyable or easier. While the objective itself might be difficult, what it will do when accomplished is make us happier or more successful or even more content. Accepting that what I have just said is true, it begs the question as to why so many resolutions go unfulfilled and unaccomplished. The same question could be asked of objectives associated with work. Why is it, if the objective, when fulfilled, will make us happier, successful or content, do so many objectives lie on the scrap heap of failure. I believe there are a number of reasons, and before we look at setting objectives in the context of appraisal and criteria-based interviewing, we will look at setting objectives in a wider setting.

Setting objectives

To introduce the reasons why I feel objectives are not reached, I want to use a well-known mnemonic, **PRAMKU**. We will look to see what each letter represents, then I will make some comments as to how failure to observe each step of the suggested process in setting objectives can contribute to failure in accomplishing the objective.

P – Precise
R – Realistic
A – Achievable
M – Measurable
K – Known
U – Understood

Precise

The suggestion here is that each of our objectives should be very precise, both in terms of quality and quantity. For example, it is not good enough to say, 'My objective this year is to do better'. What does this mean? How will you or anyone else know if you have done better? What can you compare it with? We need to identify the exact behaviour that will change and the performance that will change to make us better, i.e. the *what* and the *how*. Let us look at a few more examples to make sure that we really understand what *precise* means in terms of setting objectives. Consider this objective:

> My objective is to approach 15 more potential clients, making five extra appointments and accomplishing two extra sales every week.

Now we are getting very precise. The numbers in the objective *quantify* it, 'every week' *qualifies* it, and we can easily compare it with what is already being done because we know that at the present this particular person is making two sales per week less than is being proposed.

Consider this objective:

> My objective is to become the top salesman in the region, to make the company convention and to achieve the top honours for the year.

While there are some suggested quantifiers in this statement, it is still too vague and not precise enough. The suggested quantifiers are the company convention and the top honours. It would be a matter of record as to what the qualification for the company convention would be, so we could easily quantify what had to be achieved for this individual to attend. It is the same with top honours. The top honours would have a qualification level that could easily be identified. What the objective statement does not say is *how* all of this is to be accomplished. Therefore it is not precise enough.

All objectives, whether they are in the form of New Year Resolutions or are work related, should be very precise and should be quantifiable and qualifiable.

Realistic

My experience tells me that individuals and company bosses could share equally the criticism that too often objectives are not realistic. Sometimes, as individuals, we get caught up in the enthusiasm of setting new objectives, often an enthusiasm that sweeps away all doubt and discouragement. With all doubts gone, we feel there is not a mountain too high that we cannot climb, no obstacle so big that we cannot get around it, no challenge beyond our ability to conquer. It is in these moments that we set objectives that are beyond our capability to deliver, and when the moment of truth presents itself, we perhaps say that it was a crazy objective anyway. On the other hand, I have experienced a scenario when a company is doing badly, sales are down, costs are rising, and the powers that be demand objectives that are totally unrealistic. They impose a 20 per cent increase on a target objective that is 30 per cent down in its achievement. This means an increase in business of 50 per cent, which is, to say the least, wishing on a prayer. So we need to be realistic when we agree objectives. We need to take into account what we are accomplishing now, where we can make improvements, and what we will have to do to get any change in performance and behaviour. A good guide is to ask yourself, 'What will I have to do, that I am not doing now, to achieve this objective?' Or indeed, 'What will I have to stop doing in order to achieve the objective?' Whenever we agree to do more, be more efficient, be more effective, or change our behaviour, there is a price to pay. It may be that the price is a change of attitude, or longer hours, or more effort, or to stop doing something that we like. All of this must be considered so that the objective, when accepted, becomes totally realistic.

Achievable

You might say that if an objective is realistic it is achievable, but not necessarily. The objective might be realistic to you, but cannot be achieved because someone else or some other department or even some other company cannot keep to their end of the agreement. So often, the accomplishment of objectives depends on others as well as yourself, and not just other people you deal with. Legislation can change and make a very realistic objective no longer achievable. For example, suppose Company A has an objective to run profitably. They sit down, consult and agree expenditure against income, and work out that it is, in fact, a realistic objective. Everyone in the organisation does their bit, everyone cooperates, then two months into the financial year, with everything on target, a regulatory body imposes new legislation that will impose huge new costs. Now the objective becomes unachievable and a new one would have to be set.

Whenever we set objectives, we must explore all the hidden factors that could make the objective unachievable. Of course it is impossible to cover all eventualities, but there must come a point when we can say, 'Having taken into account all the known factors, we believe the objectives are achievable'.

Measurable

I remember asking a colleague once, 'What sort of year are you going to have?' He replied, 'A great year'. I then said, 'How are you doing to date?' He replied, 'I haven't got a clue'. I remember thinking to myself that he stood no chance of having a great year, although I suppose I should have asked what a great year looked like. What *does* a great year mean?

Objectives must be measurable, on a daily, weekly, monthly, quarterly and yearly basis. It is no good discovering in November that you are not going to achieve your objectives for a year that ends in December. By the same token, yearly objectives, broken down into monthly and weekly, thereby daily tasks, can quickly be evaluated to see whether or not some adjustment needs to be made. Measurable objectives will include who does *what* by *when* and *how*. It means that not only *can* the objective be measured, but that there is a process and system that *will* measure progress, and agreed dates that will be used to monitor progress and feedback results.

Known

Try to think of the last time that someone you know, perhaps yourself, refused to say what their New Year Resolution was. 'I'm not saying', they say, 'because I might not achieve it'. In many, many instances, such an utterance will guarantee it is not achieved. I am always amazed when I find company employees who do not know what the objectives of the company are and what the objectives of their jobs are. How can anyone set objectives to improve if they do not know on what they are improving? When we get to appraising people, it is improvement in behaviour and performance that we are looking for and so it becomes important that agreed areas for improvement (objectives) are known. The overall objectives of the job may not change from year to year, there may be only subtle changes or they only may change in terms of quantity. How the job is done is something that is constantly changing. The *how* is not only procedural. It could be the manner in which things are said and done, and once we get into the manner of things, we get into competences. I believe there is great strength in publicising an objective to improve output by adopting a different style of management and by being prepared to be evaluated by all who contribute to that output.

Understood

Misunderstanding is one of the single, biggest reasons for failing to reach objectives. Either the objective was not understood, or the role of the individual in accomplishing that objective was not understood. How many times have you heard people say, 'That was not my understanding'? I make it a habit now, when I agree objectives with anyone, that I write a letter confirming what I understood was to be accomplished.

I have used this mnemonic in countless training sessions to get minds focused on the steps that, if followed, will make the attainment of objectives a matter of course. With this broad guideline for setting objectives we are ready to see how setting objectives in relation to competences becomes an essential part of appraising performance/ behaviour. Before doing so however, here is one final piece of advice.

We do not always have the opportunity to contribute to the setting of objectives. By this I mean that the objectives for the job will have been set perhaps before we took the job. We should always have the opportunity to contribute to the objectives that will improve our performance in the job. I believe that the line manager should contribute, after all he/she will have more of the big picture and will hopefully be guiding our careers towards promotion. But the biggest contributor should be the one doing the job, providing they are not, of course, just learning the job.

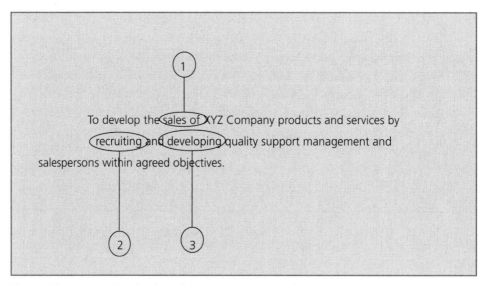

Figure 3 The three main objectives of the Branch Manager's job.

Determining key objectives

The key objectives for any job will have their roots in the job purpose statement. Once we have a clear picture of why the job exists, what has to be done to justify the job remaining becomes that much easier. Let us look at the objectives of the job separately from an individual's objectives in the job. The reason for doing this is simple. Unless the job changes, the objective of the job will remain the same, year on year. A simple example would be the job of a salesperson: the objective of the job, possibly the main one, is to sell, and that is unlikely to change. Let us look at the job purpose statement of our Branch Manager in a direct sales company, and see if we can pick out the main objectives of this job.

There are three main objectives clearly identified with this job, by which a successful manager could be measured. It is unlikely that these objectives will change unless the job changes. For example, a company may decide that all future recruitment of salespeople will be handled from Head Office. If this were to happen, then one of these objectives would disappear. What the job purpose statement does not do is to *quantify* the objectives. You might, therefore, have five different managers, all with the same job but with different *agreed objectives*. What the statement also does not do is to stipulate *how* these objectives are to be carried out. This means that individual objectives could be agreed. In fact it is from the *how* and the *quantifying* that we can start to set key objectives for the individual. These may be different each quarter or each year. I say 'may', because some key objectives may take a year or two to achieve. If for some reason all the salespeople in an office were to resign, then it could well take a couple of years for the manager to reach key objectives.

Looking again at the three main objectives of our manager's job, it is easy to see how key objectives within these three main objectives can be developed. For instance, objective number 1 is sales of the company products and services. Individual key objectives would quantify this and start to put production figures forward, not only for the year, but also measured on a weekly and monthly basis. The recruitment objective again would be quantified to create individual key objectives. These would be in the shape of manpower figures – the overall number of recruits on a monthly and yearly basis. The development objective is a little more difficult to quantify, although I suppose the number of training courses run, or field coaching visits carried out begin to set individual key objectives in this area.

But I believe that key objectives should fall into two camps: the outputs – in the case we are looking at, the sales made and the number of people recruited; and the inputs – the competences needed to produce the results. I believe very strongly that if the competences can be developed, the results will take care of themselves. So when we get round to appraising performance, I am suggesting that we appraise both the outputs (results) and the inputs (competences).

We have already discovered that there will be 12 to 15 competences, possibly more, associated with each job. Are we going to appraise all of these? The answer is yes and no. Someone who is just starting out in a new job may have a lot of developing to do in a number of competences. Those who have been in the job for a while may need to develop just a few, although if they want a bigger job they may need to develop each competence to a higher level. Whatever the scenario, it is important to avoid what is known as **over-kill**. Quite simply this is demanding too much from an individual so that in the end you get a reasonable level in a lot of competences, instead of excellence in a few. With time on our side, we should all work for excellence, working on those competences that need developing the most. This may mean setting just two to three as key objectives in a year or a quarter, developing them, reporting on them, observing them and appraising them. So, how do we know where to start?

Start by identifying the areas where the job holder makes the biggest contribution. Then identify the competences that are needed to improve or maintain that contribution. Then choose the competences that need developing the most. How do we identify the contribution areas? By going back to the job purpose statement. By identifying the objectives, we will identify the tasks that will have to be carried out to achieve the objectives. Then decide how to measure whether the contribution areas are successful or not. Then, from all of this, identify the competences and, lastly, the ones that you want to work on. The last part of the process requires both the individual and the line manager to identify and agree the competences that most need development.

Let me demonstrate with the job we are already looking at, our Branch Manager (direct sales).

BRANCH MANAGER (Direct Sales)

Objectives (contributions)	How to measure (measures)

1. Sales production

■ Premium income

2. Recruitment

■ Interview/appointment ratio
■ Number of recruits
■ Ability to source (*competence*)

3. Training & development

■ Records
■ Course attendances
■ Training logs
■ Retention (*competence*)

4. Work environment

■ Office decor & appearance
■ Motivation (*competence*)
■ Communication (*competence*)
■ Team work (*competence*)
■ Morale (*competence*)
  (the last 4 from feedback)

5. Quality control

■ Manpower (interviewing *competence*)
■ Systems control (*competence*)
■ Planning (*competence*)
■ Time management (*competence*)
■ Commitment (*competence*)

This is just a simple illustration of how, by identifying the key objectives of a job, you can identify the way to measure effectiveness, then identify some of the competences needed to do the job well. You can use this simple method for each job, and in so doing create quite a big list of competences. The job is made easy by having the list of competences ready to hand, with the definitions, so that when you identify the measures, you can also identify the competences that will be needed to produce the measures.

Just to make sure that the process is clear in the mind, let us take one objective from Fig. 3 (page 58), and apply the process through to a conclusion. Let us look at objective number 3.

Training and development

Of the four measures mentioned, i.e. records, course attendances, training logs and retention, let us look at retention. How does retention qualify as a competence, and how can you use it to measure the effectiveness of training and development? First, we need to understand that retention, used in this context, is the retaining of recruited salespersons. It means that people recruited as salespersons have stayed with the company, are progressing in their careers and are showing signs of success. With this in mind, training and development play a key role in people getting established in a new career, and therefore become very good measures for effectiveness. I remember being asked by a company to conduct a survey of 'leavers'. This was simply a questionnaire carried out over the telephone, in which people who had left the company within the first six months were asked various questions to determine why they had left. The most common reason given was the lack of management support, and this interpreted into little or no training and development on the job. So a good way to measure the effectiveness of this management objective is to test how many new recruits survive the first six months of a new career.

The second question we were asking of this measure was, 'How does it qualify as a competence?' In and of itself, it might not, but when you think of the skills needed to train and develop people, it most certainly qualifies. Here are just some of the competences that are associated with training and development:

- Motivating and developing others
- Influencing morale
- Planning
- Commitment to achieve
- Team-building
- Decision-making

- Communication/feedback
- Quality and efficiency
- Counselling
- Time management

- Empathy and understanding
- Monitoring progress
- Adaptability
- Initiative

Do you notice anything about these competences? Of course, they are all of the competences that were tested and accepted for the job of the Branch Manager in the example we are using. So you see how easy it is to look for the objectives, determine how you will measure them in terms of effectiveness, then identify the competences that will be applied to make them effective.

Equally yoked together

There is still today, in the eastern states of America, a competition between farmers which involves the yoking of oxen together and the moving of heavy loads. Like any competition of this nature, it is taken very seriously and months, if not years, of preparation go into the matching of the teams of oxen. Like the horses in the 'Ben Hur' analogy we used in Chapter 1, it is important that they work together and that they all pull in the same direction. The term used for perfect matching is 'Equally yoked together', and farmers pay a lot of money and spend a lot of time trying to get the perfect team that is equally yoked together. One of the fascinating facts about this competition is that it is not always the biggest and the strongest oxen that win. More often than not it is the team that pulls together, each doing its part but equally yoked together. So it is with any team, whether that team is at the office, on the factory floor, in the field. There are no exceptions. We want to have everyone contributing to the successful accomplishment of objectives, by all pulling in the same direction by being equally yoked together.

Apart from poor management styles, personalities and possibly a host of other excuses, the main reason why people pull in different directions is because they *think* they are going in the same direction, but are not. If we equate direction with objectives, then the reason is that objectives are not set, or are not clear, or have been misunderstood or are not measured, or are a combination of all of these.

Check your compass

I have always been impressed by the statements 'synchronise your watches' or 'check compass bearing' when watching action movies. In fact as a boy, these statements became part of the dialogue as I played out my boyhood fantasies. I wish that more company managers and executives would use these statements today and apply the principles that go with them. If they did, so much more would be accomplished. Broadly speaking, the definition of both of these statements is to work together, going in the same direction. The same direction is clearly identified in the mission statement. It can be *north* if you like, but whatever it is, everyone knows it and knows the way. We work together by reaching objectives that, like rungs on a ladder or steps in a stairway, lead upwards towards the overall objective.

One of the best analogies I ever heard illustrating the importance of the statement 'Check your compass' was in the case of an Outward Bound activity involving three teams. The overall objective was to reach a certain place in a given time, collecting information along the way, but also leaving vital information. The teams were to approach the destination from three different directions, the final destination being the same for all three teams. What they did not know was that their paths would cross at different points, and that the information that was left was vital to all the teams reaching the ultimate destination. The final counsel to each of the teams was that only when all the teams were assembled at the final destination would the exercise be complete and deemed to be a success.

Let us study this scenario for a moment and see if we can pick out some similarities between this exercise and running a business. First, each team had the same overall objective. Each team therefore became part of a larger team. Each team would have individual objectives that, when accomplished, would contribute to the larger team reaching the overall objective. Although the teams would operate with different styles and start from different positions, nevertheless they were all striving for the same destination. Each team would constantly have to check on their position and monitor it to make sure that the final destination would be reached. Each team was reliant on the other – if vital information was not left where it should have been and at the correct time, the overall objective would not be reached. Competences like commitment, reliability, initiative, planning, resilience etc. would be needed by each team, but possibly expressed at different levels. Each member of the team would have individual objectives to fulfil and each team leader would have the responsibility to see that these objectives were completed.

It really isn't difficult when you start to analyse this exercise to come up with lots and lots of similarities between the workplace and an Outward Bound project. In fact, I think some of the terminology used on these exercises would be a great advantage if used in the work environment – phrases like 'synchronise your watches' and 'check compass bearing'.

To conclude this chapter, please consider the value of setting objectives and then giving individuals the freedom to decide how they will reach them. I am not suggesting a total abdication by management, rather a more participative style of management where regular feedback and accountability will ensure that nothing drastic goes wrong. The power behind individual freedom and accountability is the rapid development of people and the harnessing of good ideas from a larger group of people. Working under one's own initiative creates more opportunity than it does potential trouble. Couple this with the individual setting his/her own objectives within the parameters of the job, and you start to have empowerment. This, in turn, means that the company's overall objectives are 'owned' by all the work force, not just management, and when that happens the results will exceed even the wildest of dreams.

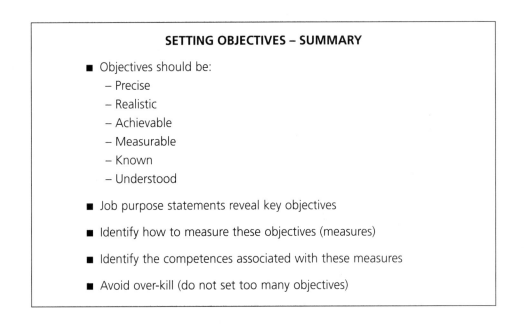

SETTING OBJECTIVES – SUMMARY

■ Objectives should be:
    – Precise
    – Realistic
    – Achievable
    – Measurable
    – Known
    – Understood

■ Job purpose statements reveal key objectives

■ Identify how to measure these objectives (measures)

■ Identify the competences associated with these measures

■ Avoid over-kill (do not set too many objectives)

CHAPTER FIVE

Measuring performance

In this chapter we examine:

- Measuring performance to bring about improvement

- How to measure performance

- Choosing the correct method

- Appraising on facts not feelings

I remember receiving an invitation through the post to be a judge at a speech festival. It was not a professional group, rather a group of young men and women who were trying to improve their ability to speak in public. My first reaction was one of pleasure, after all it would be nice to be entertained, but the more I thought about it, the more aware I became of the great responsibility. My comments, my judgements could and probably would have a great influence on all those who were to perform. These were young people, easy to upset or discourage, easy to disappoint or mislead, and I wanted to make a positive contribution to their lives and their efforts.

I cite this story for no other reason than to bring to the attention the great responsibility that comes with assessing others' performance or behaviour. Both what we say and the way that we say it can, and more often than not will, have a profound effect on those we are assessing. Perhaps we should start the appraising process by asking the question, 'Why are we appraising?'. In every instance it will be to improve performance or behaviour. Even when all the feedback is positive and complimentary, we are still seeking to encourage and to improve the performance even more.

Accepting then, that the objective of appraising and measuring performance is to get improvement, we must also accept that the responsibility for that improvement is shared. Of course the person giving the performance has a responsibility to improve, but those appraising or giving feedback also have a responsibility to assist in that improvement. Sometimes that responsibility may be no more than to give honest, objective feedback and advice in an acceptable way. Acceptable to whom? To those to whom we give the feedback. After all, of what value is feedback if it is not accepted and acted upon?

Feedback with feelings

When I was a boy of 13, I was invited to give a five-minute public speech to an audience of around 70 people. I was scared, so scared that several times I came close to calling it all off. My tutor, however, was tremendous. He helped me prepare my talk, encouraged me and believed in me. He said to me as I was about to walk to the podium, 'Just do your best and no matter what you will be a winner'. Encouraged by his remarks, I launched into my talk with enthusiasm. I watched my audience and I looked for friendly faces. Three minutes into my talk, I lost my way. Try as I might I could not find my place in my notes and I dried up. Moments of silence seemed to stretch into minutes and finally in desparation I looked up and said, 'That's all I have to say' and sat down. As I turned to leave the podium, a well-dressed woman seated in the front row said, 'Well that was a poor show, wasn't it?' I heard her. Her words cut me to the heart. How could she know how I had sweated over that talk, how could she know how hard I had worked to get it right? As I sat down, I turned to my tutor and I said, 'I will never ever speak in public again'.

Of course I have spoken publicly many times in many places throughout the world, thanks to a wise tutor who helped me put a silly comment into perspective. But what if he had not been there? What if the only feedback I had received were those words from that woman? What if the only measurement of my performance were those few words, 'Well that was a poor show, wasn't it?' Would my performance next time have been improved? Possibly, but also possibly not because there might not have been a next time.

What we say and how we say it can have the most profound effect on people. We can destroy self-esteem, discourage, or change someone's life for the worst, simply by what we say and how we say it. I am not advocating here that we lie. Sometimes the truth is hard to accept but accept it we must. I have always found that giving feedback that calls for great improvement, in other words feedback that is not so complimentary, can still be motivational to the recipient, provided I am careful about *how* I give that feedback.

Let us look at some golden rules for measuring performance that will help us get it right every time, and will ensure that those we appraise are left feeling positive and excited about getting even better.

_____ 1 _____

Identify the performance you want to measure and improve

While this may seem to be obvious, I have witnessed many times a recipient of an appraisal slump in despair, as performance has been appraised that fell outside the duties of the job. If we are going to get it right, we must first go to the job purpose statement, identify the objectives, agree the competences needed to ensure the successful accomplishment of those objectives, and then agree which of those competences we will appraise. We call this addressing the *inputs*, and this is the performance we want to measure. Get this right and the end result takes care of itself. Let us use a simple example to illustrate what is meant. Let's use a receptionist, the first person someone contacting your company will either see or speak to. The job purpose statement for this job might read:

> To promote the image of the XYZ Company by helping clients and potential clients to make contact with the relevant personnel, in an efficient, effective and helpful way.

Identifying the objectives of this job is again simple; there are three:

1 To promote the company

2 To help clients or potential clients

3 To contact the correct personnel

Next we identify the competences associated with the objectives. We can do this by drawing a bar chart listing the objectives and then some of the tasks that a receptionist will do. This, in turn, will identify the competences needed to do the job. We can then choose the competences we will measure in the performance of the job. Let us say that of all the competences we have chosen two to measure: *impact* and *listening*.

Now we need to agree how the use of these competences is going to improve performance. What will the receptionist do that is not being done now to improve impact and listening? What will she/he change? What does the company need to do? How will these changes help the overall objectives be realised? Notice that I am being very precise and specific. This is because if I am not, I might measure some other performance or behaviour that has not been agreed, and confuse and upset the receptionist when giving an appraisal. There will already be a code of practice for the receptionist laid down by the company. At some time or other someone taught that practice to the receptionist. Perhaps the interpretation put on the practice by the teacher was incorrect. The current receptionist might know a better way of doing things or, indeed, the company may decide that there is a better way of doing things. However, once you have the code of practice firmly established, and have identified the competences, and know what effective performance looks like, you can start to measure any improvement in performance and behaviour.

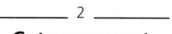

2

Get agreement

Improvement by co-operation

Some years ago I was running a course with the main objective being to improve each delegate's time management skills. One of the first things I did on the course was to ask each delegate why they were in attendance. There were varied responses. The one that really disturbed me, however, was the delegate who said, 'Because I was told to come'. When the manager of that delegate read the report I wrote on him, he would have realised that the whole principle of time management had been offended. I doubt whether there was any improvement in performance for that delegate as far as time management was concerned, but was it his fault? To get accurate readings we must use the correct tools and we must have cooperation.

There are two ways to get co-operation – by force or by agreement – and it is the willing cooperation that we want. Forced cooperation will only bring temporary improvement and while the performance might appear to improve, the morale will most certainly not. When we talk about improved performance, the inference is that the improvement will be permanent, and that even more improvement will come on top of that. Forced cooperation is likely to bring about an improvement that is in evidence only when the boss is around. If, on the other hand, the co-operation comes willingly, because the person involved can see the personal as well as the business benefits, then the improvement will not only be permanent, but the individual is likely to seek ways of improving herself/himself.

When deciding which competences are to be improved, consult the individual involved, and try to get to the situation where you are supporting her/his suggestions, rather than the other way round. This may not be easy. Some may not make suggestions, but it is possible to get agreement and cooperation through clever negotiation and counselling. The benefit of getting agreement, besides the cooperation, is the fact that the individual now expects to be measured in performance. Monitoring performance will not be seen as spying, but as personal development.

——— 3 ———
How to measure improvement

This third golden rule is a very important one because it identifies how the performance will be measured and how any improvement will be recognised. Again, get agreement as to how this is going to happen.

I don't suppose anyone really enjoys being watched as they do their job. It is like having someone looking over your shoulder, the inference being, of course, that they are looking for something that is being done incorrectly. This attitude has to change if the appraisal is to have any real meaning and significance. I actually do want someone to watch what I do, so that their observations can be objective and not just an opinion.

Feedback with evidence

Some years ago I was attending my annual appraisal with my boss. We were discussing my performance and results and he was making various comments. All was going well until we addressed the competence assertiveness, his words to me being, 'I don't think you are assertive enough'. Of course I asked him for evidence that I was not being assertive. I wanted to know upon what his opinion was based. The appraisal turned into a very heated debate as I refused to accept evaluations based on feelings or hunches. I wanted evidence and I was entitled to get it. In the end we agreed to disagree, but with me writing on the appraisal why I couldn't accept his evaluation. If my boss had been able to give me just one example of where he had witnessed me being less assertive than I ought to have been, I would have accepted his evaluation. All he needed to do was to make sure that he sat in on some of the department meetings that I chaired and witness the discussions with section heads that I had, and he would have been in a very strong position to validate his evaluation.

How we measure performance improvement has to be known, understood, accepted and agreed. We actually do want to be seen doing the job. We do not want feelings or hunches or heresay deciding how effective our performance has been. No matter how uncomfortable it is to have a boss shadow us for an hour or two, or even a day, in order to observe our performance, it is much better than having an appraisal based on feelings.

Of course there are a number of ways in which performance can be measured. I believe observation to be the most important, but let us consider some others.

1 Reports

2 Surveys

3 Feedback from collegues

4 Morale/environment

As far as reports go, they can be useful in measuring improvement, and I don't just mean results. Written reports from other sections of the company that we deal with, reports from training courses that we have attended, reports specifically identifying how we have dealt with a project and the outcomes, all help in measuring performance improvement. It is worth expanding on the training course report, since all the improvement in performance may not begin in the workplace. While the workplace will be the benefactor in the improvement, it may take a training course to identify what the improvement should look like, if only because the competence becomes better understood and the exercises on the course start the improvement process. The course report then becomes a powerful indicator of attitude and application.

Surveys of our customers, and these can be no other than the people we provide our direct service to, can be very useful. For example, going back to our receptionist, a survey around the company asking for feedback on the service provided is a sound way of measuring improvement. A telephone call into the company, without disclosing your identity, is another good indicator in the case of our receptionist. There are a lot of service industries that survey their customers, seeking feedback on the company performance as it relates to customer care. Most companies have a suggestion box or even an incentive scheme that rewards individuals for making suggestions that improve productivity or efficiency. It would be a very simple matter to design a survey sheet relating to an individual's desire to improve performance. This could then be completed by those who are most closely affected by the job being done.

Feedback from colleagues is only really valuable when it is known that this will happen, and when we can be sure of the personalities involved. When the circumstances are right, this provides a powerful method of measuring performance. When I was head of training, this was a common practice among the trainers. We would welcome a colleague sitting in on a training session and giving feedback on our performance. This feedback was all the more pertinent because it came from peers who were doing the same job. This also meant that colleagues were aware of the competences that were to be improved in an individual, and that everyone wanted to help.

I mention morale and environment because these are quickly seen and felt. An individual might come to work more smartly dressed, might display a more willing attitude, could be more cheerful etc. Being visual, the improvement becomes more obvious and tends to have a more immediate effect. I happen to believe that improved performance has a lot to do with the environment we worked in. Put someone in an office that is not conducive to improved performance (by this I mean its physical proportions) and not only will you not get improved performance but you will also get frustration, resentment and ultimately poor performance.

When I took over an old, established branch of a company some years back, the first thing I did was to change the environment to encourage efficiency, create a sense of pride and create an immediate feeling of improvement.

_____ 4 _____

Make sure you get accurate readings

To do this you have to use the correct tools to get the measurement. In the past, the favourite method used to bring about improvement was to 'send him on a course', and I am not knocking courses. As a trainer myself I know how powerful and important training courses can be, but they are not the answer to every performance improvement challenge. As important as identifying the improvement needed, and of getting the agreement that it is needed, is the need to use the correct method of bringing about that improvement.

Apart from the paper tools that can be used to measure performance, let us look at the different methods (tools) that trainers use to impart a skill or teach a principle that can motivate an idividual to want to improve.

Lectures

Sometimes it takes no more than education to bring about an improvement in performance. All that is needed is the knowledge that one can improve and some idea of how to improve, and then the improvement is self-motivated. Lectures on procedures, principles and practices can provide this knowledge, and they do not have to be 'live'. They can come in the form of audio tapes, video tapes and even written text.

Discussions

These can have the same benefits as lectures but with the added benefit of feedback and debate. It s a good practice to have the team together to discuss the way forward and debate how performance can be improved. If it is just a matter of education, and maybe a few helpful hints together with offers of help, this is a great way to get things started. If you hold regular team discussions, they will also be a good indicator for the improvement of competences, especially if the competence is something like communication, listening, assertiveness, negotiation, impact etc. It may be that you would agree that improvement in these competences will be measured by what happens in the discussion group.

Role plays

Again, role plays are an excellent forum for measuring progress and monitoring performance. So many of the competences can be observed in a role play situation that it makes this measurement tool one of the most validating. This tool does assume that the competence is known and understood, and can be applied in the workplace, so it is more than education. In fact role-playing can be the vehicle by which the skill is acquired. Such competences as communication, negotiation, assertiveness, interviewing, persuasion etc. can be measured so easily in a role play scenario. In reality, this has become a very valid alternative to observation in the workplace. So often managers tell me that observing all their direct reports in the workplace would take up more time than they can allow, so they opt for monthly role plays as part of the training and development of their people.

Business games

You don't actually have to be on a training course to experience a business game. They can be run as part of a development programme in a department and individuals can be given roles to test the competences. Do this regularly enough and performance improvement will become easy to monitor.

Projects

These can be individual and team and again they are excellent tools for measuring progress, especially when you compare the performance of one project and its outcome with another similar one. The projects should be work-related. They may be within the workplace entirely, or they can be outside the workplace, perhaps evening or weekend projects. There are a number of off-the-shelf projects that can be purchased to test competences, or you can devise your own.

Training courses

I want to mention these because they do have real value, especially if they are an off-the-shelf course designed to address a particular competence. The reality is that any course that does not get the delegates involved in the competence is merely educating/motivating. In other words, if I attend a public speaking course, and part of the course involves me giving a five-minute speech, then I am acquiring the competence or at least starting to. Residential courses tend to involve the delegates in projects, role plays and demonstrations, so they become valid in the acquiring of competences. If you use training courses, make sure that the content of the course is such that the course report will tell you what the performance of your delegate was like so that you can compare it with the performance in the workplace.

These are not all the methods trainers use but they do give an idea of the different methods that can be used to help people learn and to improve performance behaviour. However, just as people have different ways of learning, choosing the method to improve someone's performance must be individually considered. Get to know your people and you will know which method will bring about the best results. Alternatively, ask the individual which method they prefer. Of course, time and financial and personal constraints etc. will always make developing people a difficult task, but the rewards heavily outweigh the costs.

_____ 5 _____

Feelings versus hard facts

I know that I have mentioned this topic earlier but it is the centre of all that we do in appraising. It would be tragic to put the whole process in place from the mission statement down to job purpose and competences, only to have it all wasted by being appraised on feelings. Some of the people I have worked with – managers, executives and work force – have felt that this is all a waste of time, that nothing is going to change. Of course if this is their attitude and belief, they are absolutely right. Appraisals are like any job worth doing, they are worth doing right. No company can legislate for the executive or manager who has an indifferent attitude or approach, but every company can do something about it once that attitude or approach has become apparent. No self-respecting individual who wants to do a good job, who is ambitious and anxious to improve, can afford to settle for the feelings appraisal. It doesn't work even when the feelings are on your side, because sooner or later you come up against the manager who knows what he is looking for, knows how to measure performance and the use of competences, then it is often too late to do anything about it.

There is a saying that 'people who feel good about themselves produce good results'. It is a good saying and my observation is that people who feel good about themselves do so in part at least because they are well trained and well developed. They have pride not just in themselves but in the company, belief not just in themselves but in the company.

I believe that people like honesty, but not honesty that is questionable. For example, not, 'I am going to be honest with you, I feel that your performance this year has been disappointing and so I am not recommending your promotion'. But, 'If we are going to be honest with each other, your performance has not been what we expected. You were going to do such and such, but you have not. I have observed you. I have training reports on you, all of which tell us that you have not kept your side of the arrangement. What do you think this means as far as promotion is concerned?' In addition to this, of course, will be the need to produce evidence to support the observations. Producing hard facts doesn't necessarily soften the blow, but they do convey the message that there is nothing personal in the evaluation, and that the evaluation is objective and free from just gut feelings and emotions.

How are we going to measure performance?

So to conclude this chapter let me ask *how are we going to measure performance?*
Let me make a list and in summary make a few comments about each method, even though something may have already been said in the previous pages.

1 Observation on the job

2 Peer group feedback

3 Team feedback

4 Customer surveys

5 Use of meetings

6 Auditing records

7 Reports

8 Complaints

9 Results against targets

1. Observation on the job

Obviously, this is one of the most valid methods of measuring performance, yet one of the most difficult to get understanding and cooperation, more often than not because the intention is misunderstood or is treated with suspicion. As has already been said, the difficulty is also the time factor, the amount of time available to a manager or supervisor to work one-to-one with each job holder. Having said this, this method is the most valid because the evidence of performance is obtained first hand and is not clouded by heresay or another's misunderstanding. Do work at getting all those who work for you to appreciate the value of having you observe them as they perform their duties, both in the contribution you make in giving your time, and the benefit of you seeing for yourself the strengths and weaknesses of each individual. As long as weaknesses are not used to destroy self-esteem, are not used as a big stick to 'beat' people, but are used as a means of identifying development areas which, when addressed, will make the job holder better at what they do and better prepared for promotion, the on-the-job observation exercise will be a pleasure for all involved.

2. Peer group feedback

This must not be seen or understood to be a spy network and the best way to avoid this is to be upfront with the objectives of such an exercise. State from the beginning that you are not interested in tales out of school or gossip, but that you are interested in getting constructive feedback that will strengthen individuals and the team and improve performance. When I was a member of an executive group we had the policy of being asked about each other's performance. I was often asked about colleagues' performance and behaviour and they about mine. We had an honest and open policy and it worked. I was never surprised to find evidence in my annual appraisal that came from working closely with my peers. Having said this, I do appreciate that this method of measuring performance has to be handled with care and sensitivity – it is not a method that always yields the kinds of results that we want overnight.

3. Team feedback

This is especially valuable when the team has projects to work on that several of them have been involved in together. Again, this calls for open and honest evaluation of performance. As a manager, I found that this was a powerful method of getting feedback on individual performance, knowing beforehand, as I often did, the competence and the individual I wanted to assess. This method of feedback gave good indications of performance levels. There is also great merit in having the team accountable to each other. They are quick to identify where the weaknesses are being shown and by whom.

4. Customer surveys

I am really approaching this method from the angle that, in most situations, the customer might not be outside of the company. For example, in a training department the customer would be all those attending the course; in a head office environment it might be that a different department or departments would be our customers. Whoever benefits from the service we provide are our customers. Sending out a survey to our customers asking specific questions that relate to specific areas of service allows us to get some very good feedback on performance levels. Without naming names we can get a good measurement of how all the participants in our service area are performing in the eyes of our customers.

5. Use of meetings

There are a number of meetings that we might consider when evaluating this method of measuring performance. The team briefing meeting is useful for noting how the participants conduct themselves, how they respond to questions, how strongly they communicate, and how they ask questions and make suggestions. If we are measuring performance in any of the soft competences, i.e. interpersonal skills, leadership skills etc. meetings are a good method to observe and note how individuals perform.

6. Auditing records

Personnel records or personal records are useful for measuring progress and performance. If a level of performance is recorded, it provides a very useful benchmark for measuring improvement. Records of performance will identify trends and will allow the manager to identify possible cause and effect – they provide powerful facts that cannot be disputed and can be great motivators. It may be that from time to time you will want to keep records of individual meetings or conversations that you can refer to and use as a means of evaluating progress and measuring improvement.

7. Reports

These are especially valid when reporting performance-related statistics or quantifiable levels of personal involvement by the job holder. Like records, they provide benchmarks and comparisons, and as well as reporting the *outputs*, the actual results, they can be a powerful indicator for other competences such as commitment and energy.

8. Complaints

I almost hate to include this method of measurement because it implies being negative, looking for that which is wrong rather than that which is good. However, if complaint is something that is an indicator of performance, lack of complaint becomes a very positive measurement of that performance. I know of one service department that had a policy of measuring the number of complaints in order to determine the improvement of the service being offered. They even wrote into their mission statement their desire to provide a complaint-free service. If we take complaints by the scruff of the neck and determine that we will manage them and use them as a positive means of improving our performance, they become a very positive method of measuring performance.

9. Results against target

I mean this in a broader sense than quantifiable results. I mean in the achievement of any result whether it be behaviour or performance. I can set myself a target to improve my communication skills and I can measure that improvement. I would need to identify very precisely what that improvement would look like and I would need to have precise ways of measuring the improvement. With all that in place I could then use the result versus target method to record my improvement. The inference here, of course, is that I don't just say I want to improve, I clarify where my skill is at present in terms of performance, identify where I would like it to be in terms of performance, then identify what I have to do to achieve my target and monitor it.

It would be foolish to assume that these are all the methods we can use to measure performance; however they are the more well-known ones and at least show that there are many ways to measure performance and identify improvement.

MEASURING PERFORMANCE – SUMMARY

- Measuring performance is to bring about improvement

- Clearly identify the performance to be improved

- Get agreement from the individual

- Choose from a variety of methods for measuring improvement

- Get accurate feedback by choosing the correct method

- Give appraisals based on facts, not just feelings

CHAPTER SIX

Conducting
the appraisal

In this chapter we examine:

■ Creating an appraisal process

■ How to rate performance

■ The appraisal interview

■ How to give feedback

■ Eight steps to conducting appraisals

■ How to use an appraisal check list

One of the key skills in conducting the appraisal/performance management interviews is that of giving feedback. A common and often very effective method of feedback is the 360 degree appraisal. This is where the process is designed to generate feedback from various sources, i.e. from managers, peers, customers etc., the idea being to get a wide and rounded view of individual performance. It is not uncommon to give a name to these other sources, for example they can be referred to as assessors, raters, multi-raters or appraisers. How those involved in giving feedback on a 360 degree basis are used, depends on a number of factors:

1 How are they chosen/appointed?

2 How objective can they be?

3 How available are they?

Will they give feedback on all aspects of performance?

5 Will they focus on values?

How to choose appraisers

1 It is not uncommon to have those who are to be appraised identify those they wish to carry out the evaluation. The benefit of doing this is that often an appraisee can identify those individuals who are best placed to observe their performance, and give objective feedback. It is, of course, essential that those identified as possible appraisers are in a position to observe, and can give objective feedback. Generally speaking these will be individuals who work closely with the appraisee; they may serve on the same project team or be a colleague. They may be recipients of the appraisee's work, or at least be in the line of a process through which work from the appraisee will pass.

The downside to having the appraisers chosen by the appraisee is the fact that only friends or those expected to say good things about the appraisee may be identified. I believe that the identification and the appointing of appraisers is best carried out as a joint discussion between the manager and the appraisee. Another consideration is the fact those those nominated should be under no obligation to accept the opportunity.

How objective can they be?

Giving feedback on an individual performance involves more than expressing opinion; it will also require obtaining evidence to support opinion. Objectivity will arise from the evidence of the performance observed. This may be records of conversations, copies of written communications, examples of performance seen and possible testimony from third parties. The evidence supplied will depend on the performance observed and the competence or skill of the appraisee to receive feedback. Therefore it becomes essential that those chosen as appraisers know what they are giving feedback on, the specific competencies and the standard by which the evaluation will be made.

How available are they?

This really ties in with the choosing of the appraiser. There is no point in asking someone to be an appraiser if the opportunity for them to observe and collect evidence of performance is very limited.

Will they give feedback on all aspects of performance?

Generally no. It is unlikely that they are qualified to do so, and unlikely that they would have the time or inclination to do so. It is common practice to have appraisers focus on specific behaviour/performance that relate to specific competences. Remember that having many people involved in the process allows the appraisers to focus on a few specific behaviours.

Will they focus on values?

Most often this is what appraisers do. The organisation will have some values that they wish to see observed across all sections and departments; these are often referred to as general competences. They identify *how* the organisation wishes to conduct its business, and will include such things as:

- Customer focus
- Communication
- Integrity
- Planning/personal effectiveness etc.

Not all organisations will use the 360 degree method for performance management; in fact it is still more common to find the manager–appraisee method in use. Whichever method is used, the principles outlined above apply. The manager–appraisee method, however, requires the manager to take a wider look at one individual's performance.

Conducting the appraisal has as much to do with *how* it is done as *what* is done, so in this chapter we will look at both – the how and the what of criteria-based appraisals. As you read through the chapter, and the process for conducting appraisal becomes clear, so too will come suggestions as to how the appraisal can best be conducted. You will also find suggestions as to which tools (paperwork) you should use, and how to use those tools to get the best result. Remember, the underlying reason for all appraisals is to bring about an improvement in performance, to see what competences need developing and to decide how and when that development will take place.

Feedback, the breakfast of champions

Some years ago a group of my neighbours and I decided to take up golf; in fact several of us had played before, although none of us had a handicap. Of course those of us who had played before quickly asserted our dominance and took delight in beating the beginners and offering advice. Our advice was not worth anything because none of us really knew what we were talking about. One of my neighbours took the game very seriously, which in a way was unfortunate because he was probably the worst player of all. Constantly getting beaten into last place did not discourage him. In fact it had the reverse effect – he took professional lessons. He learned what he was doing wrong and he learned what he needed to do to become much better at playing golf. He looked forward to every game because it gave him the chance to practise what he had been taught, and he looked forward to every lesson because he knew that he would get a good evaluation of his game. He told me that the professional who taught him was ruthless in his evaluations, but that they were acceptable because the evaluation was based on first-hand knowledge of what was wrong and what had been agreed should be improved. My neighbour told me that he actually looked forward to being told what he had to do to improve his performance. Today, he is by far the better golfer of all those who started together.

There is a power in giving feedback and appraising performance when both the appraisee and the appraiser know what is being evaluated and the need to improve is agreed. I believe that there is a good analogy between my neighbour and his golf and giving an appraisal of performance in the workplace. If every manager approached the job of appraising and evaluating performance as the golf professional did, then enormous strides in performance improvement could be made. Of course it could be argued that my neighbour wanted to improve his game, the inference being that not everyone wants to improve in the job. I don't believe that, at least I do not believe that this is the normal way people think. I believe that everyone enjoys doing a good job and being recognised for it. This then is the power of criteria-based appraisals. They are based on real areas for improvement, real skills that will make the job holder better at what they do. The performance being appraised is not entirely based on the result, but on what went into getting the result. Criteria-based appraisals clearly identify all the skills that go into getting a result, then matches the individual performance against those skills. The matching is done through observation and reports, but reports on the behaviour, not just the result, and reports that allow behaviour and performance to be compared.

The question is asked, 'How often should one be appraised?'. The answer is, 'Continually'. This is true. There should be a continual appraisal, however it is also true that appraisals tend to take place annually. I believe that there is a strong argument that the annual appraisal should remain, but that quarterly appraisals should also be introduced. I really do not see the value in deciding at a particular time of the year, that performance has not met expectations. It is much better to agree a twelve-month objective and measure it on a quarterly basis, with the opportunity to measure on a monthly and weekly basis also. When this is done, especially the quarterly appraisal because it will often take three months to see real, permanent improvement, mistakes can be rectified and new motivation given, so that the yearly objective is more likely to be achieved.

It is also essential that the yearly expectations are recorded and the way forward clearly identified and to do this an appraisal form or booklet should be produced. The following is a suggested table of contents for an appraisal booklet which we will look at in detail. It is not exhaustive.

1 Relevant information regarding the job holder

2 A list of the key objectives agreed at the last appraisal (quarterly/annual)

3 The performance in relation to the objectives set

4 An assessment of the competences associated with the job

5 Results-orientated objectives and the related performance over the past quarter/year

6 An assessment of technical knowledge and skills, including processes

7 Factors beyond the control of the individual effecting performance

8 Development needs and aspirations

9 Development/action plans

10 The appraisee's comments on the appraisal

My purpose in giving this list is not to design a company appraisal booklet, but rather to outline some of the information which I believe is essential. Each company will know its own needs and what it requires for information in the appraisal form/booklet; however, to repeat myself, in criteria-based appraisals the information listed above is necessary.

——————— 1 ———————

Relevant information regarding the job holder

This need be no more than name, job title, how long the individual has worked in the job, and what period the appraisal is covering. It would be helpful to have a copy of the job purpose statement available (often this is printed in the appraisal booklet at the front) as it will serve as a reminder of the overall objectives of the job. The length of time that someone has worked in a job can be very indicative. If the performance by the job holder is poor, and the length of service long, it is worth exploring why this is the case. Is it because the job has changed, or because of the lack of training or perhaps poor attitude on behalf of the individual or management? The period of appraisal is important so that a new manager can get a true picture of what has been agreed and the time that has been given for that improvement to manifest itself. Another piece of information that will be useful and therefore should be available is the benchmark for each competence and the rating against that benchmark for the person being appraised. This should exist as a booklet in its own right and should be part of the personnel file for each job holder.

——————— 2 ———————

A list of the key objectives agreed at the last appraisal (quarterly/annual)

The key objectives mentioned here are not necessarily the key objectives of the job. In fact they are more likely to be competences, which, when improved, will make a significant improvement in the performance of the job. These competences would have been identified at the last appraisal and a plan of action to bring about an improvement agreed. Of course other objectives that might be regarded as *key* would be productivity-related. These too would form part of the action plan and would be recorded on the appropriate page of the appraisal booklet.

One of the first things that I would do if I were to conduct an appraisal is to review the objectives that were agreed at the last appraisal, and get renewed agreement that these are the key objectives that are to be appraised at the current appraisal. If the period being appraised is over the past quarter or year, there has been sufficient time for there to be five or six key objectives to be appraised. This will not constitute an over-kill because, as I have said, there has been a minimum of three months during which the objective can be worked on. This is especially true when the key objective is a competence because as one competence is developed, it will often impact on another. For example, supposing that one of the key objectives is *listening*. As you develop listening so do you also develop other communication skills, such as empathy and understanding. Then evaluation and judgement likewise could be developed, and so on. Having said this, it is important to remember the over-kill principle and not set too many objectives.

----------- 3 -----------

The performance in relation to the objectives set

Opposite or close to the key objectives agreed and set for the past appraisal period should be a space to report on the performance of the individual against those object-ives. This is not a numerical report (certainly not if the objective is a competence); it is written evidence identifying the level of improvement or lack of improvement. Where does this evidence come from? It comes from the observations that have been made and recorded, reports written following training courses, feedback from colleagues or customers, and all of the other ways in which performance can be measured which were discussed in the previous chapter. In the appraisal booklet it might be no more than a note referring you to a file containing more comprehensive information.

Do try to avoid using words like 'good', 'excellent' or 'much improved', as this really does not say very much because each of us has our own perception of what is good and excellent. If you must use these adjectives say why the performance was good or excellent, and say how the performance was much improved, or add the words 'see accompanying file' because that is where the evidence is. If the key objective was results-orientated, then have the performance sheets that will support the evaluation and allow a comparison between before and after to be made. Using this information is the basis of the appraisal. How well the appraisal goes depends very much on how this information is used and presented. Remember that the evaluations made on this in-formation must be supported with evidence, and that in presenting this evidence it is done in a way that is both acceptable and positively motivational.

_____ 4 _____

An assessment of the competences associated with the job

I am suggesting here that this be a numerical assessment that can range over 0–7. The reason for suggesting this range is because it fits in nicely with the ratings used to set the benchmarks. However, I strongly recommend that you avoid the need to feel that at every appraisal where the performance has improved, the rating has to go up. There is enormous scope for improvement within the bands. Improvement could and should be recognised, but without the appraiser feeling the need to move the appraisee up a band each time the competence is appraised. Let me outline the way the numerical assessment can be used, giving a short explanation, so that you can see how easily and quickly you can rate the use of a competence.

Rating scale:

0 – Not observed.   1 – High priority development needed.
2 – Development needed.   3 – Low priority development needed.
4 – Meets job requirement.   5 – Strength.
6 – Extreme strength.   7 – Performance at higher job level.

Competence	Skill demonstrated during quarter	0	1	2	3	4	5	6	7
Listening	Clarified a situation by asking open questions, feeding back the understanding and correctly diagnosing the course of action to take.						5		

A similar notation will be made for each competence associated with the job. Even though a job holder will not be working on improving every competence, it is a good practice to get an evaluation as to the level of performance of the job holder against the expectation of the job. It is from this overview that you can identify quickly those competences that are weak and need strengthening, and you can begin to agree with the job holder how the strengthening of these competences will come about. This page will also set the priorities. For instance, any competence being performed below level 4, which is the level required for the job, must constitute a priority in terms of improvement.

If a rating of 0 is used, indicating that the competence has not been observed, please do not assume that it is either a strength or a weakness. It should become a priority for observation in order that a true evaluation can be made. It ought to be unacceptable that any competence should be rated a 0 over the course of a year. If it is, the failure is with the manager not the job holder. Why? Because, as has already been discussed, there are numerous ways in which a manager can get feedback on a job holder's performance.

The short statement that constitutes the evidence for your evaluation need be no more than that. Those competences that are the agreed objectives to be improved will have further statements or reports to substantiate your evaluation for them filed elsewhere. But this short statement that indicates the level of performance must be precise and it must be accurate – no gut feelings, but real evidence to support your rating. When it is, acceptance by the job holder becomes that much easier to obtain.

———— 5 ————

Results-orientated objectives and the related performance over the past quarter/year

What this heading means is results that are quantifiable, i.e. the number of sales to be made or the number of people to recruit. These results would be numerical and would be identified both in the profit sense and in the matching of targets with actual performance. Of course if your company or department doesn't have a sales target or manpower target, you may be measuring levels of service.

In order to start to quantify a job holder's contribution, go to the job purpose statement and identify again the key objectives. Ask how these objectives can be quantified and start to build a picture of what is being achieved now. Once you can put a numerical evaluation on what is being done now, you can easily set performance figures that will show an improvement. This is how performance-related bonus schemes work and how performance-related wage increases are agreed.

Appraising numerical results is relatively easy, after all a job holder either achieved the numerical target or he/she didn't. However, of all the results-orientated appraisals that can be conducted, the numerical ones are open to abuse and I will tell you why. Too often the targets were imposed, they were not a matter of discussion nor were they PRAMKUed, i.e. measured against the mnemonic 'precise, realistic, achievable, measurable, known and understood'. Too often the target set was to satisfy a company need, a sales projection to keep the board and the shareholders happy, rather than a realistic goal that could be accomplished. Add to this the fact that the job holder knows the results before you do, so if the results are not up to expectation, the appraisal is likely to be a negative experience and not the motivator it should be.

That is the downside to appraising numerical results, but there is an upside. There are, of course, companies which do set the targets correctly and which communicate with the job holder who is encouraged to set his/her own targets. They are measured against PRAMKU and the job holder not only agrees with the target but enthusiastically goes about accomplishing it. If in this scenario the results do not match the expectation, at least the job holder expects to give an accounting and is not side-tracked with the thought that the target was unrealistic or unachievable in the first place.

I believe that as much thought and preparation need to go into appraising hard results as it does to appraise competences, perhaps more because the idea behind appraisal is to leave people feeling good about themselves. Telling job holders what they already know, especially if it is bad news and hard results, can be the greatest turn-off, takes skilful management to appraise and leaves the job holder motivated and determined to do better. It is worth remembering the statement, 'People who feel good about themselves produce good results'.

—— 6 ——
An assessment of technical knowledge and skills, including processes

In a rapidly changing business world where technology is improving in leaps and bounds, it becomes necessary to appraise every job holder periodically to evaluate how this technology and knowledge is being assimilated into the workplace. While the objectives of the job may not change so rapidly, how to do the job and the tools for doing the job certainly do. With these changes will also come different ways or processes for getting the results desired. This may mean re-training. It would be foolish of the executive and senior manager to assume that every job holder is coping with this new knowledge and technology. It makes sense to evaluate the situation with every job holder. The appraisal allows for such an evaluation, but again there is a need to be specific: not 'How are you coping?' but 'How are you applying this new knowledge?' or 'Tell me how the new process has impacted on your job'.

One of the last things I did as an employee was come to terms with the introduction of a lap-top computer designed for use at the point of sale. It did away with reams of paperwork and was designed to lead the sale. You cannot begin to imagine the difficulty that so many of the sales people had with that computer. Overnight they ceased to be open communicators who conducted sales interviews on an eye-to-eye basis. Instead they became withdrawn and clumsy in the sales interview, often losing their way and, as a result, the sale. The interesting thing about all of this was the fact that they had not lost the skill to sell, indeed the job of selling had not changed; what had changed was how the sale was to be made, or more precisely the process for getting the sale now involved technology.

Also changing might be the technical aspects of the product or service the company is marketing, and again this has to be accepted and learned. Sometimes the assessment of this knowledge is best done through examinations or training courses, but the appraisal gives a good opportunity to evaluate where the job holder is at present and where they need to go in terms of improvement. If the job holder has been required to use new or updated technology, it is quite in order at the time of appraisal to request a demonstration so that the appraiser can see for himself the understanding and application that the job holder is bringing to the job. If this is not practical because of time constraints, perhaps a demonstration during the two weeks preceding the appraisal would be more convenient. While it is not necessary to make long and copious notes regarding the technical knowledge and skill of a job holder, it is important to use the appraisal to up-date yourself as to how the job holder is coping with all the changes and applying them in the workplace. Hopefully, training courses and on-the-job training will ensure that all major changes are accepted and implemented smoothly.

_____ 7 _____

Factors beyond the control of the individual effecting performance

In any performance there are, or certainly can be, factors or circumstances beyond the control of the job holder which will influence the outcome. These should be taken into consideration when appraising and the way to do this is through discussion. Sometimes these factors will be known to the manager because thay may be factors that the company or department have introduced. A change in job or added responsibility, a change in direction, relationship problems at work, poor cooperation from another department or company, and the economic situation are all factors that can influence performance. Personal trials such as poor health or marital problems, challenges with children and family, and financial worries are also factors having an impact on performance. Much of the time, these factors may be known and built into the performance expectations for the job holder. Sometimes they are not known or can occur during the appraisal period. Whatever they are and whenever they manifest themselves, the appraisal is a time for consideration and explanation. What this section of the appraisal *is not* is a time for excuses and blaming others, and as a manager you will need to be sure that this is made clear to all those being appraised. The reality is of course that no one likes to fall short of expectations, so the opportunity to apportion blame or make excuses can look like a Godsend. I always found it useful to approach this section of the appraisal with some examples of my own. For instance, I would say, 'I know that the changing of interest rates created a strain on spendable income in the past few months, so how much of your shortfall would you put down to this?' Very rarely did any of those I was appraising apportion much to this type of factor. I found that by fronting it the appraisee was more inclined to focus on the real reasons. Do not be surprised to find that some job holders will identify you, the manager, as a factor influencing performance. It may be that you will be a positive factor, because I am not suggesting that all factors will be negative. In fact sometimes job holders will meet the performance requirements because of favourable factors, and these too need to be taken into account during the appraisal process. But now and again you may find a job holder identifying you as the factor beyond his/her control which adversely influenced performance. When this happens, the thing not to do is to get defensive. You must remain as neutral as you can, as objective as you can, and get specific evidence to support the allegation. Be prepared to listen and to accept the job holder's perception. If there is hard evidence, make a commitment to change. This is not weakness but incredible strength. I remember using such a claim against me as a trade off. I agreed that I would change if the appraisee would change, and that we would monitor each other. Not only did I get vastly improved performance, but I made a good friend as well.

8

Development needs and aspirations

It is in this section of the appraisal that you will record the agreed development needs of the appraisee – and notice that I have said *agreed*. What you do not want is a list of improvements that you have made, that you want to see implemented in the performance of the job holder, but that he or she does not agree with. Why? The answer is obvious: we want and need cooperation. This section does not identify new goals or targets, it is not to be quantified in the sense that sales quotas or service levels will be expressed numerically, rather it is the further training or on-the-job development that will take place. Nor do we have to be specific as to how that development will take place. This will come in the next section. All we do here is list those areas for development.

The use of the word aspirations in the title opens up the purpose of this section even more, for this is the opportunity for the appraisee to identify what it is that he/she wants from the career. Where do they see themselves in two, five or seven years from now? Have they career aspirations that will need training and development outside the current job specification? Do you need to identify the route to that aspiration clearly, including perhaps academic qualifications? A word of caution here because sometimes individuals have aspirations that you cannot begin to fill or that might be well beyond their ability. These too have to be discussed. Indeed, many a good appraisal turns into the beginning of a career path counselling session that clarifies and gives direction to the individual and the manager.

As well as career aspirations, it is good to discuss overall aspirations – what it is that someone wants to do with their life. They may have political ambitions that will impact on the job, perhaps positively or negatively. They may have aspirations to emigrate or work overseas. All this can be discussed. Perhaps you are thinking that no one in their right mind is going to disclose aspirations that might lead them to leaving the company or to being asked to leave the company, but my experience is that generally this is not so. When I was a boss, I wanted people with ambition and if I or the company couldn't fill that ambition then I was happy to have them make a very positive contribution for as long as it was possible. After all, the result was nearly the same. If I didn't ask and they didn't tell, their leaving was not planned for and came at the most inopportune time; whereas if it was openly discussed, they still left, but it was planned and was not inconvenient. I am not advocating that we train and develop people for others to benefit from, but the reality is that this is exactly what we all do, and I cannot see the situation changing.

I always treated this section very seriously. If a job holder has no aspirations and ambition, I would be concerned. Knowing what they are, even if it means we cannot meet those aspirations, gives us time to plan and get the best out of people in the meantime.

——— 9 ———
Development/action plans

Now we start to record precise methods of bringing about the improvement and the development we are looking for in the individual. My suggestion is that you use a page that is laid out in such a way that the development need is identified, how it is to be developed is identified along with by whom and by when. The following is an example:

Competence or knowledge to be developed	Method to be used	By whom	By when
Communication skills	Role play	Manager/ job holder	End of quarter

The whole page of your appraisal booklet could look like this with each area for development clearly identified together with the method etc. Also recorded on this page would be the action that each of us might have to take to bring about the development. For example, as the manager I might need to book a training course for the appraisee, so this would be recorded, or perhaps I might have to make some self-development materials available, then this too would be recorded. Perhaps the individual concerned would need to take an evening course to gain academic qualifications. Role plays between colleagues might have to be arranged, with days spent away from the workplace. All these sorts of arrangements are recorded here so that the job holder can see that the development is important and is going to happen.

Out of this comes a two-way commitment, real evidence of intent and a plan against which we can measure progress. Of course this page of the appraisal booklet may also be a mark of the failure of the development programme if the recorded development plan is not carried out. So both the manager and the appraisee need to be serious about what is to be done, and committed to seeing that it is carried through to completion.

I always found this part of the appraisal most gratifying. To have the enthusiastic cooperation of the appraisee in agreeing a plan of action that is going to bring about a great improvement, and to build the relationship by making a personal commitment to help in that improvement, was a motivational and satisfying exercise. The high feelings of self-worth that this exercise can bring about, together with the high morale and positive attitude, create a real buzz in the workplace and makes your office or department the place to be.

_____ 10 _____
The appraisee's comments on the appraisal

The last, but certainly not the least, step in our appraisal process gives the job holder an opportunity to comment on the appraisal. Was it considered to be fairly conducted? Was each step followed and the appropriate amount of time allocated to it? Was there evidence to support the evaluation and did the manager show any bias? These are all questions that can bring about a response from the appraisee and which can be recorded in the booklet. Again, it may be that you will get some negative remarks following your carrying out of the appraisal. Do not get defensive, nor put the appraisee under any kind of threat because of those remarks. The purpose of this section is, in part, to ensure that the appraisal is fairly conducted without bias. It may be that the appraisee will record that he/she do not agree with your assessment. I would not be concerned about this if there was evidence to support my assessment. If there was not, I might have to take an honest look at my assessment and see if I had any bias.

If I were your manager and you were appraising others, I would want to see some of the appraisals that you had carried out. I would want to look at this section to get some feedback from the appraisees. I do not say this in a threatening sense, since I believe that threats are self-defeating, but I would emphasize how important it is that appraisals are seen as real opportunities to motivate and uplift people. If they are like this now, or if they are to become like this in the future, it is you the manager that will make it so.

How to evaluate and give feedback

Now that we have been through the process of appraisal, I want to look at the important skill of evaluation and feedback and to do this I am going to use a very simple formula known as SSES.

S – Self-evaluation
S – Specific behaviour
E – Effect of that behaviour
S – Suggestions

Self-evaluation

The value that comes from allowing an individual to feed back on how they feel their performance has been greatly outweighs what some see as the disadvantages. Let us look first at the potential disadvantages or dangers so that we can get the advantages firmly in perspective.

What if the performance has been really poor? In fact, it has been so bad that there is little to find to praise in it. Some say the danger in allowing self-evaluation in these circumstances is the possibility that the job holder may say that their performance has been good or even outstanding. You then have the added problem of overcoming demotivation when your evaluation is voiced. On the other hand, you may have the situation where the performance has been good but the job holder feels thay have performed badly. If you allow self-evaluation in these circumstances you have an uphill battle to convince the job holder that they are wrong in their evaluation. The truth is, of course, that this is all nonsense. These situations may well exist whether you allow self-evaluation first or not. No matter when, or if, you allow the job holder to express their opinion of their performance, they will have an opinion and you will have to deal with it at some stage or other. I advocate that it should be up-front, allowing you to explore why they feel that way.

One of the great advantages to self-evaluation and the process that allows an individual to examine their feelings and discover evidence to support those feelings is the fact that self-discovery is far more powerful than being told. Let us examine a situation, a fictitious one but one that will allow me to demonstrate the power of self-discovery. Let us say that an individual has just answered the telephone and dealt with a customer complaint. The conversation went something like this:

Appraisee: Hello, can I help you?

Customer: I called the other day to complain and I was promised that I would be. . .

Appraisee: I'm sorry to interrupt but I think you have got through to the wrong department.

Customer: Well, who do I speak to then?

Appraisee: Who did you speak to last time you called?

Customer: I don't know. I just want this mess to be sorted out.

Appraisee: Well this is not the department you need, so I suggest you ring back when you remember who it was that you spoke to, or I can transfer you to reception.

Customer: Rings off.

Now you, as the manager, have just witnessed this conversation, hearing everything that was said. You are not happy with the way the call was handled and you want to see if you can help the job holder do it better next time. What do you do?

The easy answer is to tell the appraisee exactly what it is that you did not like and identify how you would like it done. There is nothing wrong with that, but a more powerful and lasting way to get the performance changed could come about by using SSES, and in particular step one, the self-evaluation.

Let me demonstrate by showing the following conversation that takes place between the manager and the appraisee. It takes place immediately following the conversation between the appraisee and the customer and, if it is private enough, takes place right there at the job holder's work station or, if not, in the manager's office. The required level of performance on the part of the appraisee is that he/she takes ownership of all customer complaints or queries, no matter where the matter should be referred. The customer should feel that whoever they are speaking to will take control and solve all their problems. Here then is the dialogue between the manager and the appraisee following the telephone conversation.

Manager: I wonder if we could spend a few minutes evaluating that last call. Just tell me how you felt you handled it.

Appraisee: Quite well really, after all they had got through to the wrong department.

Manager: What did you do that you particularly liked?

Appraisee: Well, I didn't lose my temper. I was quite polite.

Manager: What do you mean by *quite* polite?

Appraisee: I don't think I know what you mean.

Manager: Well, you say quite polite. What would you have had to do to be very polite?

Appraisee: I suppose I could have found out more about the complaint.

Manager: And…

Appraisee: Helped to identify the department they really needed.

Manager: And…

Appraisee: Found out the person they really needed to speak to.

Manager: You are right. If you had done that, how do you think the customer would be feeling right now?

Appraisee: Satisfied I should think.

Manager: If you were that customer how would you be feeling right now?

Appraisee: Okay, I get your point, but it isn't my job to answer customer complaints.

Manager: Isn't it?

Appraisee: I know you're back on this 'everyone owning the problem' kick, right?

Manager: So how will you handle it next time?

Appraisee: Your way.

Manager: No! Not my way. I would like you think that the person phoning in is yourself. Then answer the complaint and query as you would like your complaints and queries answered. Do you agree?

Appraisee: That's a good way of putting it, yes I do agree.

While trying to be realistic, I haven't allowed that discussion to be too difficult because I am really trying to illustrate the principle. By allowing the appraisee to discover for themselves the feelings of the customer, and in so doing feeling the same way themselves, it is more likely that in future the complaint of a customer will be handled much more effectively by this appraisee.

Specific behaviour

This is step 2 in the SSES formula and already I have identified it in the previous example. It is very important when giving feedback to focus on specific behaviour, or specific instances and examples. I can't think of many things more annoying than for someone to make an evaluation of my performance, whether good or bad, without telling me specifically what was good or bad. It is rare that the whole performance was good or bad. It is more likely that a particular behaviour or habit was good or bad. If I am going to improve my performance, I need to know which behaviour needs improving – I can't imagine that I have to change everything I am doing.

A good example would be the ice dance performed by Torvil and Dean in both the European Championships and the Winter Olympics. Getting disappointing marks in the European Championships, this great skating partnership changed some of their routine to give a better performance. They did not completely change their routine, but only the specific parts where they felt the routine was lacking. They then felt more confident about performing the routine at the Winter Olympics. I watched both of the routines, before and after, and I felt that the changes they had made visibly improved their performance very much.

So it is with every performance. If we want to improve, concentrate on specific areas, identify specific behaviour that, when changed, will bring about the desired improvement in performance. But remember the over-kill principle. Do not identify too many points for improvement and get the job holder feeling that they are not doing anything right.

Giving feedback is not just about those behaviours needing to be improved, it is also very desirable to compliment people and make them feel good about themselves. Again, the same principle applies: identify specific behaviour that can be complimented. For example, avoid saying to someone, 'That was good or excellent', but rather say, 'That was good, especially the way you handled the objection'. Now you are being specific about what was good in the performance. It will be obvious to you by now that the SSES formula works best if you have actually observed the performance yourself. It is very difficult to use SSES in a second-hand situation unless the information you have is absolutely correct. The power of feeding back to someone using the SSES formula is the fact that you have witnessed the performance first-hand, and you are therefore qualified to make an evaluation. Even if your perceptions are wrong, the person receiving the feedback and evaluation has to accept that what you are saying is based on what you saw and heard. If you are using someone else's perception, your feedback and evaluation is open to argument. Having said that, there are of course those whose opinions and evaluations you would want to consider in giving appraisal, but you would not normally attempt to use SSES while feeding back on this information – only on the behaviour expressed by the individual while you were using this information in feedback.

Effect of that behaviour

If all of us could know what effect our behaviour would have on other people, situations and results beforehand, I suspect we would all be more careful about what we said and did. When giving feedback on performance and behaviour, it is important to focus on the effect that the behaviour had on other people, situations and outcomes.

It is easy to try to excuse behaviour, to justify why we said what we did, or why we did what we did, but while we are making excuses or justification it is unlikely that our behaviour will change. We will do exactly the same again given the same circumstances. If what we said and did was wrong, or inconsiderate, or provocative in the negative sense, to keep behaving that way will not improve performance. By examining the effect of our behaviour and performance on others, we start to see things from another perspective, to feel those effects the way recipients felt them, and to see that perhaps there is a better way of handling ourselves.

For me, as a manager, to tell someone how their behaviour affected others can be very effective, and I am assuming here that the behaviour was unacceptable, but for an individual to discover this for themselves by putting themselves on the receiving end of their own behaviour, can be extremely effective. When we use the SSES formula we are identifying specific behaviour and the effect that the behaviour had on others. This is what was happening in the example used between the manager and the job holder answering the customer complaint. By getting the job holder to try to feel how the customer was feeling, the manager was able to identify the effect of behaviour on others. We do this with children all the time. How often have you said or heard it said,

'How would you feel if I did that to you?' We are trying to teach a powerful lesson to children by helping them to feel the effect of their behaviour, and this is exactly what we do when giving feedback on unacceptable behaviour.

Of course the effect of behaviour is not always negative. It can be equally powerful to have someone feel the good effects of behaviour. The benefits of this, of course, is that getting those strong warm feelings prompts an individual to want to get them again, therefore good behaviour or performance is repeated. If you have ever given a public performance in which you have excelled, stood before your audience and received rapturous applause along with shouts of delight, you know exactly what I am saying. In fact you may now be reliving that experience, feeling some of the feelings that you did then and perhaps wishing you could do it all again. This is a very powerful way in which to change behaviour or encourage its continuance, and this is what SSES is all about.

Suggestions

The final step in the formula allows for some specific suggestions to be made as to how the performance or behaviour can be improved. Oftimes these suggestions will be no more than a confirmation of what the job holder has himself/herself identified and agreed should be done. It may be that the suggestions will form part of some action plan or development plan because they will involve further training or observation. I always found that by the time I had reached this stage in the feedback evaluation interview, the way forward had been clearly identified and agreed, and it was just a matter of re-affirming the steps that needed to be taken.

Sometimes you will come across people who will not respond to the SSES formula. They may be totally uncooperative or just plain bloody minded. The skill in using the formula will depend on just how much you can get through to these people, how prepared they are to be reasonable and to listen. As with all things, so much depends on circumstance and attitude, but SSES in the hands of a skilled manager has brought many an uncooperative job holder round to reasonable discussion and response. I strongly recommend that you do not allow yourself to be discouraged from using SSES because of some early failures with uncooperative and unreasonable people.

I now want to identify some of the pitfalls in giving feedback and making evaluations. These are things to be avoided and can take the form of some golden rules of feedback and evaluation.

Golden rules of feedback and evaluation

1. Avoid feeding back on what it should have been

Your feedback must be on what you have seen and heard, not on what you would have liked to have seen and heard. There is nothing worse than to have a manager say, 'Now what you should have done . . .'. What I want to know is how can I improve what I have done? How can I learn from what I did?

2. Do not speak jargon

Quite simply this means tell me simply. Do not confuse me with jargon or language which is beyond my ability to understand.

3. Avoid feedback based just on opinion

If I hold my manager in high esteem, his opinion might be important to me, but if the manager is basing his evaluation on hard evidence, his opinion does not enter into the equation and I am bound to accept the evaluation however painful.

4. Keep the feedback/evaluation relevant

Keep the feedback relevant to the objectives agreed before the performance. If I think my manager is going to feed back on my listening skills, but he launches into my ability to communicate, I am bound to be confused.

5. Limit the feedback to something that can be actioned

There may be some physical aspect, a stammer for instance, that I cannot immediately effect. There may be circumstances over which I have little or no control. To labour feedback in these areas is ineffective because I can do little to improve them.

6. Avoid criticism

I know that it can be argued that constructive criticism is a good thing, but so often criticism is personal. Try to avoid statements like, 'That was terrible' or 'You should not have done that'.

7. Do be specific

We have already discussed the need to be specific when we identify behaviour/performance that needs improving. A general statement about the whole performance will do nothing to improve the specific behaviour that will make the difference.

8. Watch out for over-kill

Again, much has been said about feeding back too much for anyone to improve. We can cope with manageable amounts, and we are happy to do so, but feed back too much and the brain will switch off. Of all the chapters in the book perhaps this is the most important one because it involves dealing with people, it involves people skills and if we do not get these right, everything else is academic.

While the preparation and the tools we use are essential in carrying out appraisals, it is the actual appraisal and how it leaves people feeling that will make the difference. I sat in a board meeting recently when one of the executives made the following comment about appraisals. He said, 'They are a complete waste of time and money, and I do not want anyone telling me what I am doing wrong'. That is a very sad attitude and one that is totally wrong. I prefer to adopt the attitude displayed by a world religious leader when he said, 'When performance is measured, performance improves. When performance is measured and reported, the rate of improvement acccelerates.' This statement was made by Thomas S. Monson, second counsellor in the First Presidency of the Church of Jesus Christ of Latter Day Saints.

When we measure performance, that is appraisal, and when we report it, it is like giving an account, so again this is appraisal. Performance can and will improve as we encourage all those we work with to take a pride in performance by seeking to improve it. Appraisals are all about making people feel good about themselves so that their performance and behaviour improves, and the company expands its share of the market and its profits.

To conclude this chapter, let us run briefly through the steps of the appraisal from start to finish in order to ensure that everything is clear.

The eight steps to a successful appraisal

To help you, there is a check list on p. 110 that you can use to tick off items to make sure that nothing gets missed.

Step 1. Preparation is 'key'

Of course having an appraisal process in place that everyone understands is essential and it may be that some training and explanation of your process will need to be carried out before any appraisals are conducted. Make sure that everyone understands the objectives of appraisal. This means understanding why you have an appraisal process, what you hope it will achieve and how it will benefit all.

Once this is completed you can start to be more precise in your preparation. For instance, you can set the date and time for the appraisal and ensure that you have agreed these with the individual being appraised. This might mean giving plenty of notice so that the person being appraised can properly prepare himself/herself. Then make sure that you have all the relevant paperwork and evidence of performance at hand. This could be the relevant file containing training course reports or written state-ments that have been made as individual behaviour has been observed, or other pieces of feedback from colleagues who have been helping in the development of the individual being appraised. Having the appraisal booklet to hand is another important piece of preparation. Remember that this booklet will form the basis of future appraisals and will contain the information that you will record during the appraisal interview.

The place of the appraisal should be private – somewhere where open discussion and possibly disagreement can be aired without fear of interruption and being overheard. With proper planning it should always be possible to get an office or interview room, and the appraisal should be viewed with such importance that you will not settle for anything less. Once you have the room booked, how you prepare it is also important. Across-the-desk type interviews are not what appraisals are. Sitting side by side or around a round table will produce a more relaxed atmosphere. If a round table is not available, arrange the seating so that at the very least you are sitting across a corner of a desk or table. It is important that you can both see clearly any written reports or paperwork of reference, and indeed there will be times when you may want to read it together. All of the relevant paperwork should be neatly arranged on the table or desk you will use. Try to avoid hiding it or putting it on the floor. If everything is in the open, it indicates an open and honest presentation of facts that are there to help all those involved.

Another small but important point, is the lighting of the room. Whether you are using natural light or electric light, it must be sufficient and you should arrange things so that neither one of you feel uncomfortable because of too much light in the eyes or too little light to see properly. Prepare yourself by being prepared. What you have to hand will be the tools that you can use during the appraisal. If you have forgotten something, it can result in a negative appraisal. One final point regarding interruptions – there should not be any. You should not allow for any, under any circumstances – no telephones and no physical interruptions by anyone. If you have to unplug the telephone, do it. If you can arrange for a 'do not disturb' notice on the door, do it. At the very least, tell your secretary no interruptions.

Step 2. Putting the appraisee at ease opens up the conversation

Start the appraisal by putting the appraisee at ease – this is not a grilling or a telling-off opportunity. We actually want job holders to feel positive about appraisal. We want them to feel that it is in everyone's interest. Show some genuine interest in the job holder and help them feel at ease. At the same time, try to avoid small talk that will only serve to make both parties more nervous. One of the ways to avoid embarrassment and awkward silences is to explain up-front what it is that you will do. Explain the appraisal process and the booklet you will use, and how you will be taking notes that will form part of the next appraisal. Invite the appraisee to take notes of their own. Explain that they may see the notes that you have taken. Then introduce them to the objectives that were set at the previous appraisal and get them to agree that these are, in reality, what were agreed. If you are conducting the very first appraisal, explain the purpose of setting objectives and how these objectives will serve to focus the efforts of both parties in the improvement of performance, then set and agree the objectives to be reviewed at the next appraisal. Identify the areas of improvement that were agreed at the last appraisal and how that improvement was to be measured, then move into evaluating the performance, producing all the evidence to support your evaluation. Once you have evaluated the objectives set at the last appraisal you can move to Step 3.

Step 3. 'Tune in' by making sure the appraisee understands the competences

Now you are going to review all the competences that are associated with the job. This is an opportunity for you and the appraisee to make sure that there is a common understanding of what the competence means, i.e. a clear definition, and that the appraisee understands the level of performance that the job requires, i.e. the benchmark or anchor point. You can also agree an overall evaluation of these skills and whether they constitute a need for further development. This will also give you an opportunity to confirm the objectives for the next appraisal period with the appraisee. By using the rating scale already explained in this chapter, this exercise is quite easy to complete. However, getting agreement may take longer if you have no evidence to support your rating. Do remember to have the anchor points for the job with you when you review the competences. If you remember, the anchor points are the levels of performance that describe the minimum standard set for the job that is being done. Sometimes, individuals might not have reached that minimum standard or indeed they may have fallen below it in the performance of their job. By having the anchor points clearly identifiable you can start to prioritise the objectives for the coming period of appraisal. You can have these anchor points printed up in the form of a handout, or they can form part of the appraisal booklet. Make sure that you are familiar with the levels of perform-ance both above and below the anchor points, so that if you are asked what needs to be done to move up a band in performance, you can clearly explain and identify specific behaviours.

Step 4. Evaluate the 'quantifiables'

This step involves the evaluation of the numerical or quantifiable targets that have been set over the appraisal period. They may be sales targets or manpower targets, the number of items to be produced or service levels to be increased. Again, the agreed target will be measured against actual performance attained, so it is important to have all the relevant data close at hand. If the appraisee is below target, they will know that long before the appraisal interview takes place. This is why it is important to remind yourself that the appraisal gives the opportunity to discover why the results are not up to expectations, especially if it is because of the lack of training or development. Do avoid using the appraisal interview as an opportunity to reprimand as this should have taken place already if it is appropriate. By identifying shortfalls in performance during the appraisal interview, we are looking for opportunities to train and develop, and to make sure that any shortfall that is a result of the lack of knowledge or skill is properly addressed. There is always a danger when appraising results that too much emphasis is placed on them, and while this is understandable because we all know that it is results that pay the salary, try to remember that the results take care of themselves when the inputs are correct, and appraisal is more about inputs than outputs.

Step 5. Understanding the 'technical knowledge and skills' of the job

You then move on to the section covering technical knowledge and skills, including the systems and the processes. This is more of a conversation inviting the job holder to identify any real problems, or for you to feed back on examination results etc. In the ever-changing workplace where technology is playing a bigger and more important role, and where individuals may be undergoing training to do a bigger and better job, this section becomes very relevant. If new technology has been introduced and if individuals are undergoing training and experiencing some difficulty, this section of the appraisal interview gives an opportunity for the individual to comment on those difficulties and how they see them impacting on performance. This section also allows opportunity to identify further training needs and to agree an action plan to meet those needs. If an individual is struggling with new equipment or technology of any sort, this part of the appraisal interview can be a life saver.

Step 6. Examining factors outside of individual control

Once you have completed the evaluation of performance, you allow the appraisee to comment on those factors that have influenced their performance which have been outside their control. Remember that this is not an excuse-making exercise. It is an opportunity for honesty and feedback, and the opportunity for you, the manager, to understand what the appraisee feels are real obstacles to improved performance. Do not undervalue this important step, or fail to grasp its opportunities. Mankind, by nature, will always seek to lay the blame for poor performance at the feet of someone or something else, and sometimes it is correct. It is here that you might discover that you, the manager, are seen to be an obstacle to good performance. You may discover that the way you do your job is seen as a hindrance. Of course there may be factors such as illness or broken relationships that have contributed to poor performance, or it may be trouble with the law or individuals within the working environment. Identifying these factors allow you to create a plan of action to correct the situation as far as is possible, or indeed you may realise that counselling by a higher or more competent authority is needed. Please remember that most people will not divulge this sort of information willingly or readily. Some may be afraid to speak out for fear of reprisals or fear that promotion may be blocked, and some may feel that they can handle their own problems and do not want everyone else to know about them. Perhaps it is a fear of the lack of confidentiality that will restrain the individual. Whatever it is, perseverence and the building of relationships based on honesty and trust will bring about an ever-increasing discussion on these factors as time goes on.

Step 7. Agree the development needed and write an action plan

From here you move to agreeing the development needs and the plan of action to bring that development about. Explore career aspirations and agree the competences that will have to be acquired or honed in order for the aspiration to become a reality, and agree specific methods to ensure the competences are acquired or honed. It can be argued that this is what appraisal is all about, the agreeing of specific development needs and a plan of action that will turn them into reality. Do make sure that when you agree development needs and the action plan, it is a plan that can be actioned. By this I mean make sure that all the individuals involved are willing and that there are no budgetary restraints that will delay or cancel your plan. Individuals being appraised will get very excited about development if they believe it is in their interests as well as the organisation's and that the plan will happen. Try not to get drawn into making a commitment for development that is expensive or time-absorbing, when the same development could have taken place on the job. It can be argued that the best development takes place on the job and therefore most of the improvement in the performance of individuals can be brought about as they carry out the every-day functions of the job.

Step 8. Getting feedback on your, the appraiser's, performance

This brings you to the page in the booklet that allows the appraisee to make comments on the appraisal, how it was carried out and how fair they believe it to be. Do insist that the appraisee makes a comment or two, not because you are looking for praise, but because honest feedback on your performance will help you to improve also. Throughout the appraisal you will be giving and receiving feedback this is because the appraisal is a discussion and you do want a free exchange of thought and opinion. If you follow this process and use the tools I have suggested, the appraisal will be a positive experience for you and the appraisee. There is no substitute for experience and the more appraisals you conduct correctly, the more expert you will become and the more improvement in individuals will you see. One last thing to do in order to complete Step 8 is to have the individual sign off all that you have agreed. Putting one's signature to a piece of paper is powerful evidence of commitment and it also indicates agreement. Your signature also indicates commitment and allows the appraisee to feel that all that has transpired is meaningful and is to be taken seriously. Follow-up to the interview might involve a letter to the appraisee expressing thanks and reconfirming what was agreed by both parties. It might also confirm that training courses have been booked or that conversations with others involved in the development plan have taken place.

APPRAISAL CHECK LIST

Preparation before the interview	Yes	No
1 The purpose and objectives of the appraisal are understood by all?	☐	☐
2 The date and time of the interview is agreed with the appraisee?	☐	☐
3 All paperwork, files and the appraisal booklet are to hand?	☐	☐
4 The office/room has been booked?	☐	☐
5 The office/room has been set up with emphasis on lighting, seating arrangements etc.?	☐	☐
6 A 'do not disturb' sign is on the door, the telephone is disconnected, and your secretary is informed of no interruptions?	☐	☐
7 Writing pads, pens etc. are all arranged?	☐	☐

The interview		
1 Explain the process – put the appraisee at ease.	☐	☐
2 Identify and agree the objectives to be appraised.	☐	☐
3 Evaluate competences and check understanding.	☐	☐
4 Evaluate quantifiable results and agree an action plan.	☐	☐
5 Set and agree the objectives for the next appraisal period.	☐	☐
6 Test understanding and the application of technical skills.	☐	☐
7 Invite comment on factors outside of appraisee's control.	☐	☐
8 Agree the appraisee's development needs.	☐	☐
9 Agree and write up an action plan.	☐	☐
10 Invite comment from the appraisee on the interview.	☐	☐
11 Follow-up the interview by letter to all those involved.	☐	☐

CONDUCTING THE APPRAISAL – SUMMARY

- Appraising has as much to do with *how* as *what* you do.

- Appraisal is about measuring performance in order to improve it

- Create a booklet for appraisal and let it include:
  - Relevant information about the job holder
  - A list of key objectives agreed at the last appraisal
  - Performance in relation to the objective
  - An overall assessment of the competences associated with the job
  - Results-orientated objectives and performance
  - Assessment of technical knowledge
  - Factors outside the appraisee's control
  - Development needs and aspirations
  - Development action plans
  - The appraisee's comments on the appraisal

- There are enormous benefits to evaluation and feedback using the SSES formula

- Avoid the dangers by following the golden rules of feedback and evaluation

- Conduct the appraisal using the logical steps recommended

- Use a check list to avoid mistakes

CHAPTER SEVEN

Personal development and action plans

In this chapter we examine:

- What are personal development plans?

- How to create personal development plans

- Creating action plans

- Career development planning

- Handling disagreement

- Maintaining good working relationships

As soon as we use the term 'personal development' the inference is that whatever method of improvement we decide to use, it will be tailored to individual needs. Even though several individuals may be involved in the same improvement method, because we will personalise the development by setting individual objectives, the plan will be personal. The power behind the word personal comes from both the appraiser and the appraisee: from the appraiser because the strong inference is that the plan will be individually tailored, taking into consideration personal ability, personal aspirations and personal accountability; from the appraisee because the feelings being encouraged are that he/she, as an individual, is appreciated, valued, is receiving individual attention and is making a real contribution to the organisation.

If, following the appraisal, nothing happens and the whole process was no more than the appraisor taking a lot of notes and asking a lot of questions, then the fault must lie with the manager. For the appraisal and, in particular the personal development plans, must be more than intentions, promises, hopes and note-taking.

To help focus on the importance of personal development plans and action, let us consider the seven golden rules which should be followed when writing personal development plans.

1 Consider the individual for whom the plan is being written

2 Consider all the options and methods for improving performance

3 Consider the current demands and constraints

4 Make sure the plan is realistic

5 Know what the desired outcome looks like

6 Determine how you will measure the improvement

7 Give feedback regularly

Let us consider each of these rules to ensure that we understand what they are telling us.

_____ 1 _____

Consider the individual for whom the plan is being written

When considering individual development plans we must take into account physical and mental ability as well as personality traits. What will work for one often does not work for another, so when we identify a need it is not always as simple as prescribing a general course of action to improve it. Some years ago I was impressed by a manager who wanted to send a delegate to a course I was running. He called me, not to discuss the course content, but to ask who else was attending the course. He wanted to make sure that his delegate would fit in with the rest and would respond well to the other personalities on the course. Of course this is not always practical and, if external courses are being used probably, not even feasible. However, the principle of considering personality when putting together a personal development plan is recommended.

It is also recommended that we consider the mental ability of those we are trying to help improve. I have seen countless hours wasted because a delegate was not capable of keeping up, or because they responded negatively to the method being used. Knowing your people will enable you to take all these things into consideration and will ensure that the desired outcome is achieved through a pleasant experience. It is worth noting that what is available in terms of development opportunities may not be the answer, or may not meet the requirements you are looking for. Do not fall into the trap of thinking that something is better than nothing. If the method on offer does not meet the need, it is better to wait until you can create a method or find a suitable one.

_____ 2 _____

Consider all the options and methods for improving performance

It will have been seen from the previous chapters that there are a number of training methods that can be used to improve performance. Those that have been identified do not represent every method or option open to those who want to improve their per-formance. My experience in my own personal development revolves around training courses. As I was learning and attempting to improve my performance, it seems that every manager I had resorted to the old cop-out, 'send him on a course'. Consequently, I attended some very good training courses, but I have to say that I didn't need half the training I got, or more accurately the training was not relevant to the particular development need that I had at the time. Making a list of all the options and methods available to develop individuals will enable the manager to be focused and to home-in on specific needs, the likely cost of the development and, of course, to identify the desired outcome. Sometimes, because of demands or constraints, the best method or the most desirable option will not be able to be used. As frustrating as this may be, at least by knowing all the options available you can choose the next best method to bring about the desired improvement.

_____ 3 _____

Consider the current demands and constraints

One of the advantages that come with management is the opportunity to be better informed and to see more of the 'big picture'. By this I mean that perspective is enlarged by more information and wider communication channels. Receiving information on a 'need to know' basis can be restrictive when trying to understand some of the decisions that are being made by senior management. This is why derogatory remarks are often made about management decisions by those who are not privy to information. Knowing the demands and contraints, whether they be financial, political, time, resource or any other, helps the manager choose the appropriate option or method when considering the personal development of staff. Being aware of the demands and constraints will prevent embarrassment, conflict and the waste of valuable time. Let me illustrate what I mean with the following example.

Be aware of the demands and constraints

During a period of falling sales, all departments in a company were asked to restrict expenditure in order to preserve jobs. Budgets were slashed and in some cases wiped out overnight. However, one manager refused to accept the situation and, as a consequence, caused himself a lot of embarrassment. He had just completed an appraisal with a member of his staff and had agreed a development plan which involved the staff member enrolling on a very expensive week-long external training course. The course was booked and a deposit was requested to confirm the booking. This request found its way to the desk of the company training director. Knowing of the financial restrictions he queried the booking and advised that it be cancelled and re-scheduled when the financial situation improved. His recommendation was upheld by the sales director and the manager concerned was instructed to inform the staff member and the training company involved. Obviously this caused some bad feelings and some embarrassment, all of which could have been avoided if the manager had considered the contraints when agreeing a development plan with his member of staff.

––––––––– 4 –––––––––
Make sure the plan is realistic

When agreeing a development plan there are two points worth consideration: individual capability and resource availability. Individual capability extends beyond the capacity to learn and individual physical ability, and should take into consideration the family situation, financial costs and time contraints etc. If the development plan includes external training courses or courses run after normal working hours, then the family situation must be considered. External courses, while costing nothing to the individual in terms of fees, accommodation and meals etc., will require the delegate to have some money for after training hours. Delegates do have times when they meet socially and of course this involves some expense.

Another consideration if you are thinking of courses to bring about the improvement in behaviour, is the overall content of the course. Do not send a delegate on a course if the whole of the content does not contribute to improved behaviour or performance. Do consider very carefully the physical capabilities of all those whose performance you are seeking to improve. Some people may not be able to bring about the improvement because of a physical disability, or they may require some very specialised training. Whatever method you use, there will be an expectation from both the manager and the delegate. Do make sure that your expectations are valid because the method you choose will realistically deliver the improvement. Do also check resource availability: finances, internal training resources, external training resources, staff available for mentoring and coaching etc.

5

Know what the desired outcome looks like

Whenever we seek to improve performance we must have a clear picture of what the improvement will look like. It is very easy when we measure performance that is quantifiable. For example, if you want to improve sales from five to seven per week, the difference and the measurement is easy. But how do you measure an individual's ability to communicate better, or make better decisions, especially if those giving the performance have a different understanding of what is expected from those who are appraising it? Not only must there be a common understanding between appraiser and appraisee, but each must have a clear picture of what the desired performance improvement will look like.

To achieve this the objectives must be quantified as far as possible. For example, an objective stating 'To improve in decision making' is not good enough. What we want is 'To be able to make day-to-day decisions easily and, by applying the decision-making process, demonstrate the ability to contribute to bigger and more important decisions'. What the latter objective tells us is that, as a result of personal development, a manager will be able to observe the appraisee using a decision-making process while contributing to the deciding of wider and more important issues. As long as the appraiser and the appraisee have a clear picture of what the desired performance looks like, both will know when the objective is reached.

———— 6 ————
Determine how you will measure the improvement

Once we know what we are looking for we must determine how we will measure its accomplishment. The following are just a few suggestions to help illustrate how we can measure performance improvement:

■ Personal observation (remember to note the differences seen)

■ Course reports

■ Examination results

■ Feedback from colleagues

There are other considerations as well that will aid in the measurement:

■ Determine over what period of time the improvement will be measured

■ Determine how the improvement will be recorded

■ Determine when the improvement will be appraised

Once you have a clear picture of what it is that you want to see in terms of improvement, the way you will measure it will become that much easier to identify.

———— 7 ————
Give feedback regularly

Feedback measures, redirects, motivates and recommits an individual who is trying to improve performance. Of course it depends on how the feedback is given and what the feedback is, but even bad news can be given in such a way as to bring about a greater determination to improve. By giving feedback on a regular basis incorrect behaviour can be changed before it becomes a habit. Regular feedback demonstrates interest and commitment by the appraiser to the appraisee. It demonstrates a real desire on the part of the appraiser to assist in the perfomance improvement, and calls for a greater degree of accountability from the appraisee. Feedback does not always have to be carried out on a formal basis. In fact, frequent informal feedback often has a greater effect than infrequent formal feedback.

Action plans

These are really no more than a 'what, by whom and by when'. Part of the development plan will be the need to record what is going to be done, who is going to do it and by when it will be done. Adding these columns to the plan gives the opportunity to check that something is happening and that those involved are doing what they said would be done.

Career development planning

Up to now we have discussed improving performance as it relates to a particular job, but there is a wider issue: how does an individual prepare to do a better or bigger job? While most people are happy to put their feet on the first rung of the ladder, it is also known that there are other rungs ultimately leading upwards to more responsibility and financial reward. Career development planning is sensitive because many times it will mean redirecting expectations towards a more realistic future. Many times I have had staff whose aspirations have led them towards a career path that they were clearly unsuited for. Often we find that staff have the same expectations. In other words they all want to be the boss, or they all want the next rung up the ladder at the same time. Planning an individual's career development is more than who gets where the fastest. In fact, I have used the story of the tortoise and the hare to good effect on many occasions. Finding out what people want from their career is a must, and the earlier the better. Once you know what their expectations are, and you are satisfied that what is wanted is within the ability of the individual, you can start to plan the route for them. Here are some simple rules to follow:

1 Discuss career aspirations early with your staff.

2 Know what qualifications, both academic and personal, are needed in order to get to the ultimate destination.

3 Know what the time frame for getting what is wanted is.

4 Do not be afraid to redirect aspirations.

5 Do spell out the cost in terms of study and improvement.

6 Do not give promises you cannot keep.

7 Be prepared to lose some good people who are impatient to achieve.

8 Set out clearly a route for each staff member to achieve their aspirations.

9 Be prepared to change the plan if redirection is indicated.

Follow these simple rules and career development planning should be relatively easy, and appraising performance a part of a logical sequence of events. Quarterly and annual appraisals should be part of an overall career development plan and the appraisee should be able to recognise that they are on track to achieving a long-term goal.

Handling disagreement

Throughout this chapter the word *agreed* has been used whenever I have referred to development needs and personal development plans. Sometimes getting agreement is not easy – in fact we can find that far from getting agreement we are handling conflict and disagreement. There are some simple rules, which, when applied, will help resolve differences and keep the communication channels open.

Rule 1. The what versus the who

What is right will always be more important than *who* is right. Sometimes it will be personality that will trigger conflict – perhaps we do not like the way something is said or the way an instruction is given. Perhaps it will be mannerisms or a perceived lack of courtesy, or it might just be that we do not like the person or people we are dealing with. Even those we do like can provoke disagreement if we feel that they are being discourteous or are using insensitive behaviour. The trouble is that as soon as our feelings are hurt, *what* is right ceases to be of importance and instead it becomes a matter of *who* gets the upper hand. If we are the boss, getting the upper hand becomes a matter of position, power and authority, or it can do, and the cost in terms of cooperation when we take such action is high. In all disagreements try to separate personal feelings from what is right, debate the *what* and avoid letting the issue become a personal one. Sometimes what is right will be a matter of opinion and indeed, if it is, then all opinions should be considered. Opinion is shaped by what we know, what we have experienced, our values and standards and the environment, so it stands to reason that there will be a variance of opinion. As long as those we negotiate with believe that we are driven by what we believe is right, disagreements can be brought into harmony.

Rule 2. Value others' opinions

Whenever we start to value something we introduce respect, and in valuing others' opinions we will maintain an attitude of respect. This means that we will preserve individual dignity and not seek to destroy self-esteem or feelings of self-worth. As soon as we consider ourselves better than another and start to behave in a superior way, we will fall into the trap of devaluing others' contributions, opinions, accomplishments and potential, and disagreement then becomes personal. When that happens we win battles and lose wars.

Rule 3. Use your ears and your mouth in the proportion that you have them

Whenever we find ourselves in disagreement it is natural to want to put our case as strongly and as effectively as possible. There is nothing wrong with this. In fact, to keep our opinion to ourselves and quietly boil over achieves nothing. However, as strongly as we might feel, it is arrogant to think that no one else has anything worthwhile to say and to proceed to ignore any other contribution to the debate. The real strength in handling disagreement is in being able to listen to what others have to say, taking all the positive aspects of their argument to strengthen your own and then to present a well-prepared and thought out solution to the issue being debated. By listening to others you should try to see things as they see them. Try to understand why they feel the way they do, and try to answer the question, 'If I were them, would I feel the same way?'

Rule 4. Let your behaviour be the pattern for gaining agreement

Whenever we feel strongly about an issue there is a tendency to let emotion into the debate. For some reason it seems that emotion encourages loud talking, sometimes even shouting, and it is thought that he who shouts the loudest gets the decision. Have you ever tried shouting when the person you are debating with stays calm and collected and talks quietly? It is infectious. Some years ago I had an irate gentleman focus his anger on me. He shouted and he banged tables. After a while I asked him why he was shouting. I went on to say that I was surprised that a man of his background could not debate an issue calmly and collectively. It took him completely by surprise. He was used to reaction and he could not understand why I was not shouting back. My approach ruined his argument – he couldn't debate without shouting. Maintaining a quiet dignity while positively putting forward your ideas, will gain far more success than shouting and behaving like a hooligan. You will find that those you are in disagreement with will largely follow your own behaviour.

Using these four principles will allow you to debate development programmes and precise behaviours for improvement without destroying the all important need to maintain working relationships. You may not always get the agreement you look for, but if you apply these principles you will get far more agreement than disagreement.

A hypothetical appraisal

To conclude this chapter we will work through a hypothetical appraisal, focusing on the point in the appraisal when a personal development plan is to be agreed and actioned. We will use a supervisor who manages six people and who has ambitions to move up the ladder to a senior management position within the next two years. Having reviewed performance over the past year and having evaluated the results, three competence objectives have been agreed for the coming year. These are:

- Time management
- Assertiveness
- Writing reports

What we now have to do is write these objectives in a way that will be quantifiable, so that they can be easily measured and so that the method of improvement can be agreed.

Time management

The objective is: To better understand the principles of time management as they relate to prioritising events and organizing others.

Methods we will use to achieve this objective:

1 Attend a one-day time management training course to understand the principles.

2 Review the course with the manager and agree to use daily priority sheets.

3 Review the priority sheets on a weekly basis, or more often if necessary.

4 Identify a particular project that can be used to apply the new knowledge and skills obtained.

How will we measure progress?

1 Manager will test understanding of principles following the training course.

2 Weekly review of the daily priority sheets.

3 Greater productivity over the year, but on a monthly basis.

4 Feedback from those who work in the department.

What overall improvement in time management are we looking for and how will we recognise it when it is achieved?

1 Better personal organisation in terms of task management and use of personnel.

2 More productive use of the time available, resulting in improved productivity.

3 Good feedback from the staff about the way the department is organised.

4 Suggestions as to how further improvements can be made.

Assertiveness

The objective is: To display greater assertiveness in meetings by coming prepared to make a contribution and then speaking up; to take a stronger approach in calling for an accountability from the staff in the department.

Methods we will use to achieve this objective:

1 One-to-one training meetings for 30 minutes each week with the manager on preparing for meetings.

2 Identifying specific objectives for each member of staff on a daily/weekly basis and discussing them with the manager.

3 Role play accountability interviews with the manager.

4 Initiate regular meetings with staff on a one-to-one basis to call for accountability and give feedback.

How will we measure progress?

1 Monitor the weekly training meetings and give feedback.

2 Monitor the role plays and give feedback.

3 Monitor the weekly accountability meetings and have the manager sit in for one or two.

What overall improvement in assertiveness are we looking for and how will we recognise it when it is achieved?

1 Better participation in meetings, making a positive contribution that can be recognised by the manager.

2 Observed accountability from staff in the meeting of objectives.

Writing reports

The objective is: To write more comprehensive reports that identify challenges and the remedial action taken; to give senior management a better understanding of the needs of the department and a feel for what is happening at grass-roots level.

Methods we will use to achieve this objective:

1 Enroll in the report-writing course offered by the human resources department.

2 Review the course report with the manager.

3 Monitor the next three reports, discussing with the manager.

How will we measure progress?

1 Monitor reports for the remainder of the year getting feedback from the manager.

What overall improvement in writing reports are we looking for and how will we recognise it when it is achieved?

1 Better prepared reports that give the information needed by senior management in a way that allows them to keep all circumstances in perspective. The manager will give feedback when this is happening.

Now that we have all this information in the form of a development plan, we need to identify who will do what by when, and it might look something like this:

Manager: Now that we have agreed precise objectives, we need to establish a time frame and agree who will do what. For example, I will arrange the courses and will report back to you within two weeks. We also need to agree and set a time on a weekly basis for me to spend 30 minutes with you to train you in writing reports. I would like you to go away and think things through and come back to me with proposed times and days when we can meet to take care of the training, review the priority sheets and do some role plays. You also will need to identify the specific objectives for each member of your staff and initiate all the meetings you are to have with your staff for accountability. Let us agree to meet in a couple of days to report on what we have done and to set precise dates.

It is important that each task that is identified in the method to be used for improvement should be written up in an action plan to make sure that this is more than just a chat. Another step in the process is to tie all of this improvement into the career aspirations of the appraisee. It would be helpful to have the job description of the next position up the line so that the key tasks and the competences can be discussed with the appraisee. Once the improvement we are looking for is identified, not just as increasing production but as a real attempt to prepare individuals for promotion and to do a bigger job, real cooperation becomes that much easier to obtain.

It is worth noting that people do respond well to personal development. Increasingly, as I have interviewed individuals over the years, I have been asked about training and career development. It is almost as if people are asking whether or not the company is just interested in using people, with no intention of developing them to be able to do greater things. While income will always be a matter of interest to the work force, I am enthused by the increasing interest that individuals are showing in what the organisation can and will do to develop the talents they have.

As with anything else that has real value, personal development is very emotive and so it is important to approach it with care. Do not make promises that cannot be kept and do not agree development methods that need another person's approval until you have that approval. Do not be afraid to go back to those you work with and explain new constraints and make necessary changes. Of course there will be disappointment, but personal development isn't merely a sweetener.

PERSONAL DEVELOPMENT AND ACTION PLANS – SUMMARY

- Personal development plans are individual

- There are seven golden rules to writing development plans

- Action plans ensure that the *what* gets done by the *who* by the *when*

- Career development planning is long-term planning

- There are nine rules to follow when career planning

- Handling disagreement is a management skill

- Adhering to the principles will ensure agreement and maintain working relationships

---

CHAPTER EIGHT

Building on loyalty

In this chapter we examine:

- What is an 'I care' programme?

- What are the benefits?

- How to create an 'I care' environment

- How the 'I care' philosophy builds loyalty

An 'I care' programme is a concept that can have extraordinary effects both on individuals and whole organisations. It starts from the top and cascades down throughout the organisation touching everyone and everything. It even affects those who visit the organisation, whether they are clients, or those who want to do business with the company. It must start at the top and not from the bottom, simply because the basis of the concept is to lift individuals and raise self-esteem, and you have to be above someone in order to lift them up – of course, I am talking in terms of position elevation and not personal standing.

An 'I care' programme has a process and the first step is to establish a correct attitude. The correct attitude is established by evaluating behaviour at all levels and determining how we, as individuals, would like to be treated. For example, suppose I were to visit your company. What is it that would impress me about the people who work there, and what would influence me to want to do business with you time and time again? Let us work through a scenario of an exploratory visit to see how a company operates. Let us say that I am representing two groups of people: the first, those who might do business with the company; the second those who might want to work for the company. For the purpose of this exercise I am assuming that attitude influences behaviour – in other words, the attitude comes first and the behaviour reflects the attitude. I am coming unannounced in order to catch people behaving as they normally would.

First impressions form fast, fade slow

My first contact with your company will be as I try to park my car. I discover a barrier and beside it a little intercom with clear instructions to press a button for attention. I press the button and my first 'people contact' with your company has started. A voice says 'Good morning and welcome to XYZ Company. Would you please state your name and the person you are visiting.' I am impressed. Someone, and as yet I do not know who, is being very pleasant and is making me feel good. I answer the request and the conversation continues, 'Please park your car and come to reception. If you have any difficulty please come back to the intercom and let me know so that I can be of assistance.' By now I am more than impressed – I am astonished. Someone really cares about me. They do not know me but I am being treated as though I were someone really important. I park my car and find my way to reception which, by the way, is very easy because someone has taken the trouble to mark the direction clearly from every row in which cars are parked.

I enter the reception area and approach the desk. There is one receptionist who is speaking on the telephone. She looks at me, smiles and says into the telephone, 'Excuse me for one second, I have someone at reception'. She then turns to me and says, 'I will be with you in a moment sir, please take a seat'. Again I am impressed, I have not been ignored and the reality is that whoever is talking on the telephone has been treated well, so we are both feeling good. The receptionist finishes her conversation and then calls to me. She says, 'Sorry to keep you sir, can I help you?'. I tell her whom I have come to see and she asks me if I am expected. I tell her no. She then explains that she will call the person concerned and arrange for his secretary to come down and see me to either escort me to the office, or to make another arrangement. She further tells me that I can either take a seat or wait by the desk. In a few moments a secretary arrives, introduces herself and invites me to accompany her to the office where I am to meet her boss.

I think that this scenario has gone far enough to enable me to make some interesting points and to establish the process for creating an 'I care' programme. From the moment I arrived at the company I began to get messages that were telling me I was important. If I perceive that you think I am important, I also perceive that you care about me. Intercoms are so impersonal, or they can be, but not the one in my little scenario because the person behind the intercom cared. First, I was greeted and invited to say who I was – not the other way round which is so often the case. In fact, more often than not we are not greeted at all. I was invited to park my car but was then reassured that if I had any difficulty someone cared; all I had to do was go back to the intercom.

Second, I arrive at reception where I expect to be ignored if someone is talking on the telephone. But no! The receptionist acknowledges me and invites me to wait. When she comes back to me she apologises and then makes me feel important by arranging for someone to come and meet me. Can you imagine how I am feeling? The messages that have been sent all positively tell me that someone cares. Such messages must emanate from the top and they must start from the attitude that we will care and we will structure our behaviour to show that we care. So three points are worthy of consideration:

1 The 'I care' attitude

2 The 'I care' physical arrangements

3 The 'I care' behaviour

Let us talk through each point and clarify what each statement is saying, and further explore how to install this programme into any company.

_____ 1 _____
The 'I care' attitude

When we consistently display a caring attitude towards others it is because we know that they, in turn, care about us. Caring is not just an action, it is an emotion. Just imagine how you would feel if someone you care about suddenly revealed that they no longer care for you. Hopelessness and despair are products of feeling that nobody cares, and when we feel that way our attitude changes. We say to ourselves, if you do not care, then I will not care. Transfer these feelings away from individuals and into the work environment and the result can be just as negative. The fact is, we rarely feel that organisations do not care without identifying someone in that organisation on whom we can focus our frustration and anger. However, we say 'they' do not care, and only identify individuals when we are pressed. 'They' become the company or the organisation. So 'caring' seems almost to be reciprocal. We care if we feel others care. The key, of course, is to get others to care because we do. This is why I have said that the 'I care' process must work from the top downwards.

Why bother? ... Why not?

If you have ever travelled on the London Underground's Central Line out of Liverpool Street Station towards Ilford, you will be aware that shortly after leaving Stratford Station, and again going underground, you emerge above ground to travel through Leyton and Leytonstone. I have always thought that this seems to be a very run down part of east London and that the homes seem to be in need of some restoration. On the back of one of the houses, the owner has painted in large letters and in purple paint, the words 'Why Bother'. I have pondered in my mind why someone would do such a thing. What depths of despair someone would have to reach, what feelings that 'nobody cares' someone would have to have in order to display such an attitude. I am confident that it is the feeling that no one else seems to bother or care that has led the owner of the house to go to such lengths to express his frustration. Now we might say that nobody needs to feel that way, we can determine what our attitude will be, we do not have to be reactive, we can decide to be caring in spite of what others might do. Of course, if we were to say this, we would be right, but it is not so easy to do as it is to say.

Further to my story regarding the houseowner and his painted message, it was of great interest to me to see that his neighbour had responded to this message of despair by writing on his house in equally large letters and in white paint, the words, 'Why Not'. So obviously he was able to keep a fairly positive attitude to the whole situation.

But getting back to an 'I care' programme, it starts with senior management agreeing that the attitude of the company will be a caring one, and that this attitude will be most forcefully displayed by the senior management group. It will be reflected in:

■ Dress

■ Speech

■ Behaviour (time keeping, reliability, assuming responsibility etc.)

■ Communication

■ Interpersonal relationships

■ Decisions

■ Career development

■ Service, etc.

What we are saying here is that in everything we do, we will be sending out the message 'I care about you'. This means that even when reprimanding, the message is, 'I cannot accept your behaviour/performance, but I do accept you'.

This sort of attitude goes further than dealing with people; it also embraces problems and challenges. It is so easy for anyone to say when a difficult task is thrust upon them, 'That's not my job' or 'I'm busy' or 'I can't do it now'. The 'I care' programme works because everyone owns the problem or task or job, and each in turn considers themselves responsible for doing everything possible to see that the problem, task or job gets done. More will be said about this when we get to addressing the 'I care' behaviour.

2

The 'I care' physical arrangements

The 'I care' programme has to be more than an attitude, it must also be reflected in the decor and office layout. It must be reflected in the physical conditions in which people work and in which people deal with the organisation. This does not mean that everyone who works for the company has a palatial office or, indeed, that everyone has exactly the same facilities, although we are all entitled to the same facilities, for example, staff toilets and rest rooms as well as refreshment facilities. While there may be a difference in the quality of each, nevertheless each person working for the company should have access to these facilities and at the very least they should be of a decent quality.

Do keep in mind how an employee or a visitor might begin to assess whether or not the company cares. It is not simply a matter of financial reward or of financial fairness. After all, an employee will always feel that they are entitled to whatever they might be paid, if only for the work that they have done to earn it. The conditions that people work in, and are expected to work in, is a direct reflection of how important they are seen to be, how important the job they do is seen to be, and how much senior management care about both.

People in cupboards behave like mice

I remember an instance when I was involved with a school. It concerned the bursar's office or should I say cupboard, for that is what it was like. The school was about to appoint its first bursar and had advertised the position widely. Being involved with the school, I recommended that the bursar be given a new office and that the existing one be used only until something more suitable could be found. I further recommended that during the interview process when the office facility was mentioned that it was also mentioned that better accommodation was to be provided. Well the new bursar was appointed but the subject of new accommodation was never far from her mind, and she commented to me on several occasions about the inadequacy of the existing office. Of course she eventually got the new office that was promised but this example just confirmed to me once again how the physical facility is perceived as a measurement for the importance of the job and the person doing the job.

Working conditions are one thing, but another consideration is the decor of the facility that will be frequented by our customers. Clean and tidy is the least expectation. It doesn't have to be new or even the best, but it must certainly be clean.

Do I want to pay to go somewhere dirty?

Recently my son obtained free tickets for a small family circus and we agreed to go together as a family. It was obvious that the circus was hard pressed for cash even though the performance was a good one and the performers often excellent. Two things made a negative impression on me, and they were things that could have so easily been put right. First, the circus was held in a meadow and the circus ring laid out in the meadow. There was nothing wrong with this except that the grass was about six inches long. How easy it would have been to cut the grass, and what a different message the circus owners would have sent out if they had. The second thing was the circus tent itself: it was filthy and I do mean on the inside. Honest hard work would have cleaned it easily and would have sent out a far different message from the one I received, namely that they didn't care.

Everyone has a perception of their worth or value either at work, at home or in the community. There are certain places I would not go – restaurants I would not eat in, cinemas I would not frequent, etc. Why? Because they are beneath the standards I have set for myself and they would devalue my sense of self-worth. So it is at work. Send out messages that the people who work for you are perceived by the management as not being worth much, and what you are really saying is 'We don't care about you'.

Of course, 'I care' physical arrangements extend beyond the workplace and include the equipment or tools that are given to get the job done. How often I have heard someone say, 'They want the job done perfectly, but look what they have given me to work with'. It is messages again. The message that I receive may not be the one intended, but if I perceive that someone does not care as much as I do, I can be tempted to perform below the standard required. We are back to the 'If they do not care, why should I?' and this attitude is all too common.

So physical facilities send out messages of 'I care', the tools and equipment I use send out messages of 'I care', and if the quality of care is obvious, then we can expect that same amount of care in return. In reality, it is my experience that the smallest token of 'I Care' that comes from management is reciprocated 100-fold by the staff and manifests itself not only in greater productivity, but also greater cooperation, suggestions on how to improve, greater flexibility and increased morale. To summarise, it is important to remember that it is easy to say 'I care' but it is more difficult to show it consistently, and it is showing it consistently that constitutes the 'I care' programme. This programme is not a 'quick fix' or a 'here today gone tomorrow' type process. It is a 'here to stay' programme and the pay-back is huge. No matter what the situation is now in terms of physical facilities, something can be done now to show that the management cares. Whether is a coat of paint, or better equipment or even the promise of better equipment with, of course, a date for delivery, management can start to send out 'I care' messages.

I care, do you?

One of my friends did no more than to have some badges made with the inscription 'I care' in bold letters. He wore one and started to behave as though he really meant it. He gave one to everyone who showed an interest and they too started to behave as though they really meant it. Pretty soon his department became known as the department who cared, and visitors to head office made a point of visiting his floor to see if it were true.

3
The 'I care' behaviour

For behaviour to have a lasting effect, certainly in the positive sense, behaviour has to be observed over a long period of time. For example, I have often heard people say, 'Enjoy his good mood while it lasts, because it won't last for long'. If we are to have an 'I care' attitude and this is to have an effect on our behaviour, we must think in the long term, and we must not enter into this programme with conditions. In other words, it must not be a 'I'll try if you try' scenario, but rather it must be a total commitment with no conditions. It will not be easy and there will be times when others will fail you and you will fail them. That is why it is important to recognise that if the programme has merit, you do not give up. Just as a common cold is infectious, so is being an 'I care' person and it is infectious because people respond to kindness far more quickly than they do to abuse, certainly in a positive sense.

While the company or senior management might give some guidelines as to expected behaviour, and certainly this would be helpful if behaviour has to change dramatically, by and large when people grasp that the basic concept of the 'I care' programme is to treat others as they would like to treated, behaviour will be self-induced. However, to help illustrate what behaviour in an 'I care' environment looks like, let me give some precise guidance.

1. Countenance

In an 'I care' environment, self is put below the needs of others, so the countenance will always be a cheerful one. The smiling face and a cheerful approach is the order of the day, and this means everyone. Of course some people will feel uncomfortable trying to wear a smile all day, and in reality this may not be feasible, but whenever we interact with another, then the countenance should be a cheerful one.

2. Courtesy

This will include the way we talk to each other, in other words the language we use, as well as treating each other with respect. There seems to be a feeling in some organisations that you talk down to people, or that you get the best out of people by shouting at them, or a good swear at someone will do the trick. There is no room for such behaviour or sentiment in the 'I care' programme. Of course people will need to be corrected and reprimanded, but when we care about the individual, we keep our remarks centred on their performance/behaviour and not on the person. I can remember being reprimanded by a senior executive for over an hour. I remember walking from his office thinking to myself that this was the first time I had ever been told off and felt really good about it.

Courtesy, of course, includes saying 'Good morning' to people and if you are a manager who cares, you do not miss out anyone. It includes listening to others and not cutting them off. It means treating an individual as though what they have to say is important to you. It means encouraging participation in making suggestions or debate, and not treating any suggestion as though it was a waste of time. Again, it comes down to treating others as we ourselves would like to be treated, but giving it a name: 'I care'.

3. Behaviour

As already mentioned, the behaviour I refer to includes time-keeping, reliability and taking responsibility. I cannot think of too many ways to tell someone that they are not important to me or that as far as they are concerned I don't care, than for me to be late for their meetings or to not keep appointments on time. Failing to meet deadlines or schedules because of a tardy attitude or application of skill is definitely not part of the 'I care' programme. This is, of course closely tied in with reliability and doing what we say we will do. Broken promises and unkept commitments are evidence that we do not care and so our behaviour in the 'I care' programme must be the opposite. It means that we are careful about the commitments we make so that whatever we commit to, we deliver. Everyone we associate with knows we care because we do what we say we will do, we are where we are supposed to be when we are supposed to be, and management and colleagues know that we can be relied on. When we become good time-keepers, make commitments that we keep, i.e. become reliable, then we become responsible. However, responsibility, in the sense that I use it here, means much more and I would prefer to use the term 'ownership'. What I mean is we take ownership of every problem and challenge, even if they have nothing to do with the job we are doing, once we become involved with them. This may mean no more than a misdirected telephone call that puts us into contact with someone needing help. Then, what may be another's responsibility becomes our responsibility, because we care. To illustrate consider the following example:

I visit your company offices and manage to get myself lost on the third floor when I need to get to the sixth floor. It is then that I bump into you. I explain who I am and tell you that I need a certain manager. You recognise the name and tell me that his office is on the sixth floor and that the lifts are just around the corner. So far you have been polite and you have been courteous, but you haven't lived up to the 'I care' code. To do this you would not only tell me where his office is, but you would offer to take me there and, indeed, introduce me to the manager I was to meet.

Owning the problem means that you take on the responsibility for solving the problem. You do not just point out how it may be solved, but you get involved and see it through to conclusion if that is what is needed. In the 'I care' programme everyone gets involved and what is my problem becomes your problem once you become exposed to the problem. We do not say, 'Oh well, it's not my problem' – we can never walk away and feel comfortable if we know that we could have done something to help, but didn't.

In an 'I care' environment it is difficult for 'politics' to thrive, especially if everyone is committed to the programme. By politics, I mean the back-stabbing and the walking all over people. In this sense the 'I care' programme becomes a little idealistic because ambitious people will always look for opportunities to promote themselves over others. However, it would be wrong to suppose that an 'I care' programme would therefore not work. My experience is that whatever level of caring a company is able to achieve, it is much better than not having a known, specific programme of care in which individuals are made to feel good about themselves and in which the image of the company is improved.

Nowhere will the 'I care' programme have greater effect than during appraisals, for it is here that commitments are made to help individuals, and it is here that we evaluate performance with all the sensitivities that this involves. If we are known to care as managers, the appraisal becomes a pleasure. Gone are the suspicion and fear and in comes the open discussion and cooperation that we want the appraisal to be. If the company is seen and known to be a caring organisation, in times of crisis or need the workforce will repay that caring with a caring of their own. Many times, I have seen individuals assume responsibility for tasks and jobs that they do not like, simply because they see that the company or a manager needs help. At appraisal times I have witnessed individuals accept and agree to courses of action that they would normally do their utmost to avoid, because they can see that it is in their interests and the company's interests to do them, and because they work for a manager who cares and a company that cares and they know it.

I have outlined the attitudes and behaviour that are needed if an 'I care' programme is to work; now it would be useful to suggest a precise process for implementing such a programme.

The Steps towards implementing an 'I care' programme

Step 1 is to agree to an 'I care' programme at a senior management level and to see how it compliments the company mission statement.

Step 2 is to identify precise behaviours that will support the 'I care' concept. These will vary from company to company but should include how the telephone is answered, how visitors are treated, how the workforce will treat each other, etc.

Step 3 is to agree the 'ownership' concept and how it relates to the 'I care' programme.

Step 4 is to communicate the concept to all levels of the organisation.

Step 5 is for senior management to alter their behaviour if necessary in order to set the example and take the lead.

Step 6 is to agree and communicate how the programme is to be monitored.

Step 7 is to implement the programme and start to monitor it.

Step 8 is to review the programme constantly and to communicate the successes and the benefits of working in an 'I care' programme to everyone.

My experience tells me that people leave companies for only one or two reasons: either they are unfulfilled, in other words they lack job satisfaction; or they lack the necessary financial rewards. There may be other reasons such as illness or relocation, but generally speaking the main reasons are either finance or lack of fulfilment. The 'I care' programme is all about fulfilment – being wanted, appreciated and feeling important. It is about getting the best out of people by helping them to feel good about themselves and getting the best out of customers because they feel a loyalty for the company. More and more often these days, people want more than value for money in the sense of what it costs. They want value for money in terms of service and after-sales care. They want to know that if they have a complaint someone will not only listen, they will care, and in caring something positive will be done that is in the interests of all concerned. It may be that the answer that comes will not give the outcome required, but how that answer comes may well decide whether that individual or company ever does business with us again.

BUILDING ON LOYALTY – SUMMARY

- An 'I care' programme is a concept that must originate at the top

- It starts with attitude, wanting to care about the company and all associated with it

- It embraces all the physical aspects, from premises to equipment, that make people feel good

- It examines behaviour as this relates to conduct, speech and 'owning' the problem

- There is a process for implementing an 'I care' programme

- An 'I care' programme builds on loyalty and creates loyalty

---

CHAPTER NINE

Happiness is pulling together

In this chapter we examine:

- Communicating the vision

- Vision – strategy – and appraisals

- Making appraisal work.

Of all the management methods, styles and practices, the one that must incite the most distaste has to be 'mushroom management'. This is where everyone is kept in the dark and fed manure. This type of management feeds on secrecy and keeping people ill informed, and thrives on the fact that the management knows what is wanted and that that is all that matters. It stifles innovation, kills incentive and guarantees that the workforce see no further than the precise job that they do. In other words they have no idea how they are contributing to the finished product. It is not so many years ago that this style of management was the way to do things – it was the norm. Fortunately this has changed and now we enjoy a much more open style where there is a free exchange of information and much more correlation between departments and individuals. It is my opinion that while we have moved a long way from mushroom management, there is still some way to go before we maximise the potential of every worker by allowing them to see 'the big picture'.

What does my bit do?

Years ago when I started in engineering, I spent some years in the moulding shop. Here we made various components that, when assembled, would make up some complicated piece of machinery. Often the 20 to 30 moulders would be working on making parts for a number of different machines so there would be no correlation between what one was doing and another. Many times I wondered what the function would be of the parts I moulded, although in the end the mouldings I made became an end in themselves, and I ceased to have an interest in how they would function outside the environment I was working in. One day I was invited to visit the company that had placed the order for the components that I was moulding. The purpose of the visit was to see how my work was contributing to the creations of this company and how the parts I moulded fitted into the finished machine. I was fascinated. I had no idea how important my work was until I saw my work as part of a larger and more important piece of machinery. That visit changed my attitude and my work ethic. While I worked well before, now I worked with greater care and pride in what I was doing.

I learned a valuable lesson. When we can see how our work contributes to the whole, when we can see the difference that our work can make, when individuals are allowed to see the 'big picture', attitude, quality and perceptions of self-worth are all increased.

Bully Bloggs rides again

Recently I attended a board meeting where one of the directors responsible for a very important project reported his concern and dismay over the fact that he was not getting the support and the resources he needed to produce the required results. His report was an emotional one and one in which he pleaded for help and understanding and he finished his report with a personal plea that his concerns be taken seriously and as a matter of urgency. Questions were invited and although it was generally known what his project was, there was some ignorance as to who was supposed to be giving the support and who was to supply the resource. It quickly became obvious that the help he needed rested with middle management working in a number of company locations. I asked him if he had communicated his problem to them, if he had presented it to them as he had presented it to us. He responded that he had not. I asked him what it was that he was looking for and his response to this question was typical: 'I want' he said, 'a direction from the board to these managers that they must give me what I need'.

I can imagine how those managers would feel if such a directive had been given. Put yourself in their position for a moment and see if you can understand the feelings such a directive would invoke. Here you are, a manager, doing what you believe is a good job.

You have no idea that anything is wrong and suddenly out of the blue you get this directive from the board that you are to be more cooperative, and that you must respond to the demands or needs of this director. Never mind your individual circumstances, never mind the current contraints you may be working under, here you have a blanket directive. How would you feel?

Well fortunately, such a directive was not sent because a suggestion was made that was more acceptable. This was to call a meeting of all the managers concerned and to outline to them the precise nature of the problem. Then these managers were asked to consider how they could contribute to solving the problem. By sharing with them the nature of the problem and allowing them to see it in a wider context, the input and initiative they showed in dealing with it was exciting. Not only was the problem solved, but executive management discovered a huge strength and resource that they did not know existed, namely a very competent group of middle managers who, when given the 'big picture', were capable of contributing to and making sound problem-solving decisions outside their normal sphere of work.

Seeing the 'big picture'

It all comes down to whether individuals feel that they are contributing to something bigger than the immediate job they are working on. It means that the purpose of the company is known, understood and accepted, and that within that understanding there is a freedom to contribute that crosses departmental organisational or hierarchical lines. This is what empowerment is all about. It is giving individuals the freedom to deal with problems and situations as they occur. But if this is to be successful, then every individual must have a clear understanding of how that problem or situation will affect the company, how it will impact on customer service, or sales, and this means that everyone who is capable must be given the 'big picture'. Does this mean that everyone, in effect, has the same authority? Of course not. Having the 'big picture' gives an individual greater freedom to work within the constraints of the job to be done. It allows greater freedom to communicate across all levels of administration, but of course it does not give someone authority to make decisions outside of their job role.

Hierarchical processes will mean that in order for an individual to expand his/her range of authority, he/she will have to gain a promotion. I believe that by using a more open style of management we encourage individuals to expand the job role. In other words, to grow the job, to make what they do more important. Giving individuals more information and a greater perspective of what is trying to be achieved encourages them to look beyond the bounds that the job sets and to see opportunities that have always been there, but that have perhaps been missed in the past.

Communicating the vision

Another word we can use to replace the phrase 'big picture' is 'vision'. Words associated with vision include insight, imagination and dream, and of course everyone is capable of having vision. Vision is limited only by knowledge – the greater the knowledge, the more the ability to have the vision – and I am assuming that the ability to understand the knowledge is in an individual. Why does the Chief Executive Officer get the vision for the company? Because he has a deep understanding of what the purpose of the company is and what the shareholders want. He knows financial contraints and market trends, and he has a team of specialists who bring him information so that he can take account of problems and challenges and see the way ahead. But the vision is not limited to the CEO. Wherever we work in an organisation we can get a vision of the way forward in our job role or department. When we can communicate that vision to all those who will contribute to its accomplishment, get their cooperation and harness their enthusiasm, then we have synergy. However, it is the communication of vision that can be so difficult. It is one thing for a manager to see the way forward, but it is quite another to have the ability to share that vision and to get those you work with as excited as you are. One of the ways that we can share vision and get input from all those we work with is to inform. It is this free exchange of information and not keeping people in the dark, helping others to understand as much as we do or even to understand more than we do, that encourages initiative and innovation.

Failure to communicate the vision often results in uncooperative behaviour, suspicion, duplication of effort and poor output. I have seen a number of good managers get the vision and then charge off at a rate of knots leaving everyone in their wake wondering what is going on. Far from contributing to greater efficiency and effectiveness, this type of behaviour has the reverse effect. One of the best-known and best-appreciated visionaries was Martin Luther King and his great speech about his dream. The phrase 'I have a dream' has become a catch phrase and many men and women have learned what it means to be able to see clearly the way ahead and to have a dream. Today, Martin Luther King's dream has become a reality, but not before it became the dream of hundreds and thousands of both black and white people who caught his vision. Only then did the dream become a reality.

I make no apology for using such an emotive example. I believe that getting this vision into a company is an emotive issue. There will always be those who will not want to share in the vision. These may be individuals who want no more than to do a job and go home. But the vast majority of those who work in an organisation will respond to the opportunity to share in the vision, especially if they are then given the freedom to make an individual contribution to the way the vision is realised.

Having the vision will not answer all the questions as to how the vision is to be realised. Knowing where you want to be in terms of business progress is one thing, but knowing how to get there is another. You cannot begin your journey unless you know the destination, so the vision comes first. The strength of sharing the vision comes by allowing everyone else to know the destination and to contribute to the route to be taken to get you there. It also comes by acknowledging that everyone has a valuable contribution to make and allowing them to make that contribution. A good analogy comes from the merchant navy: a captain of the largest ship may sail that ship for thousands of miles, but when he gets close to the port of his destination, others, usually pilots, take over his ship to navigate it into port. Everyone in the organisation is, in effect, a pilot. By recognising the valuable contribution they make and allowing them to appreciate the contribution they make, the whole organisation benefits. I know of several companies that use a suggestion box to encourage input from the work force. In fact, they offer cash prizes for those suggestions which, when implemented, result in greater service or profitability for the company. This is proving an excellent way of getting input from the work force as to how the vision of the company can be realised while at the same time raising self-esteem among the work force through recognition and reward. However, I have also experienced where the same input has resulted because individuals felt a pride in the company and wanted to make any contribution that would improve productivity or service, with no reward sought.

Matching appraisals to business strategy

We have almost come full circle when we talk of matching appraisals with business strategy because we return to the need of knowing what the company wants to achieve and then making sure that we have the right people to bring about that achievement. If the organisation we work with is large enough, we can implement succession planning and usually we can start to identify the individuals we want from within the organisation. Otherwise we would have to look outside the organisation for the recruitment of personnel, and usually this is not succession planning but rather responding to need. Succession planning is all about identifying individuals who, with training and development, are capable of doing a bigger job. We then match the individual skills with the skills of the job to be done and we have a bank of workers that we can consider for promotion or replacement when the situation allows. How is this done? Quite simply by having an effective appraisal system that identifies each job purpose, sets the competences for the job, puts into place the key performance indicators, and then appraises individual skills on a regular basis to match resources with needs. This can be monitored on a database and can even be used in a program that will do the matching for you. Let me explain.

Once the competences are set for each of the jobs in the company and the benchmarks set for each level of performance, how the job should be performed is now a matter of record. Appraising individual performance against known criteria and a benchmark of standards becomes relatively easy. All of this information can be stored on a computer program and updated each quarter and year as jobs change or roles change. The next thing to do is to record the name of each person working in the company and evaluate their performance in the competences for their job. Now it is very easy to match the job expectations of performance in the competences with the actual performance of the individual. Since all jobs at all levels are recorded, it is easy to match an individual against any of the jobs programmed. For example, if I know that in two years' time I will need two more managers, I can match any individual performance against the job profile of the job of manager. I can see the shortfalls and I can see easily what development I would need to apply to these individuals in order to have them competent in the role of a manager in two years' time. The same applies to any job in the organisation. Succession planning becomes a very real possibility with this system and, of course, the appraisal now takes on a much higher priority because the information gained from the appraisal will up-date the system. There were a number of times when I found this system to be of great advantage, especially when I was responsible for management development with a large company. With all the information fed into the computer from the appraisals, it was so easy to identify development needs and tailor the training programmes accordingly. In addition, I worked very closely with managers in succession planning, identifying individuals and planning their development to meet future needs. Appraisals became a major contributor to this planning

Table 1 Reasons for introducing performance appraisal.

Reasons	Number of companies
Bring cultural change	48
Quality initiative	33
Improve performance	75
For pay reviews	38
Succession planning	49
Identify training needs	80
Encourage manager/worker dialogue	68
Prelude to disciplinary action	14
Reduce role of collective bargaining	3
Recruit/retain problems	18

for it was here that strengths and weaknesses were recorded and future opportunities identified. It made all of the senior managers more appreciative of what the appraisal was for and what it could do, and focused the mind on the real purpose of appraisal – that of developing people to give greater service to the organisation.

Recently, a survey was published in *IRS Employment Trends* which looked at the reasons why appraisals were held. I found the findings fascinating and I have reproduced some of the data in order to make some observations. Of the 107 organisations which responded to the questionnaire on appraisal and individual performance pay, the majority (88 per cent) used an appraisal system for some or all of their employees. I was particularly interested in why the appraisals were held and those participating responded to ten possible reasons with, of course, the right to choose any number of reasons why a performance appraisal should be used. I was also very interested in how the appraisal results were monitored, and in the impact of the appraisal itself, i.e. what were the benefits to the company, the employee, etc.

Table 1 shows the information without naming the companies who participated or the type of business they are involved in. For my purposes this information is not necessary; I am more interested in *why* an appraisal, on *what* basis, and what the perceived benefits are.

How interesting it is to note that the three most popular reasons for introducing performance appraisals have their roots in communication and development of the individual. But to what end? There is a strong suggestion that improved performance in the job is the motivator for having an appraisal, and I would not disagree with this. However, I would like to see how the appraisal was being conducted. In Chapter 6 we discussed the fact that the *how* of the appraisal is as important as the *what* of the appraisal. While the appraisal might be used to improve performance, did it result in an improvement in performance?' Table 2 tells us the answer to this question. I also found the dialogue or communication figures of interest because I have already stated that the appraisal should be a discussion. Again we can ask, 'Were the lines of communication improved because of the appraisal? Again, Table 2 gives us the answer. While the succession planning attracted a response from 49 of the 107 companies, I find it interesting that the rest did not see appraisals as a resource to aid planning for the future. I believe that they are missing out on a valuable opportunity for developing and motivating the work force by not identifying appraisals as a means of succession planning.

The two biggest benefits from conducting performance appraisals, as shown in Table 2, are improved performance and communication, with 54 and 50 companies respectively indicating these as a benefit. I believe that the commitment of employees is a natural benefit if the appraisal is seen as worthwhile and having real meaning.

Of course we cannot draw too many conclusions from these figures'because there are so many unanswered questions; questions like, 'What form of appraisal is used?', 'Is the appraisal conducted against a specific known job purpose statement that identifies the competences and the key performance indicators?', 'How many of the appraisals had personal objectives for performance improvement that were being monitored?', 'Who conducted the appraisals and were they seen as a benefit or a threat?'.

Table 2 Impact of appraisal.

Results	Number of companies
Improved individual performance	54
Improved corporate performance	33
Increased productivity	21
Increased employee commitment	39
Improved employee communications	50

Some of these questions were answered in the survey, some were not, but the figures that I have used do identify some interesting attitudes and we can draw the conclusion that, of the benefits listed, there is a strong argument that appraisals are valuable to a company even if they do not meet all the criteria I have identified in this book.

I think there are good reasons for conducting an employee survey to ask them what they think of appraisals, whether they believe they are important or not, and what they see as the benefits of appraisals to them as employees. I have already indicated in Chapter 6 that I recommend that a section of the appraisal should allow for input and feedback from the appraisee so that benefits and value are identified on both sides of the equation. Of course in an ideal situation, a benefit to the company will be seen as a benefit to the employee and vice versa, but we do not live in an ideal world so there will always be men and women who will look only for what is good for them.

Whenever we start talking about guarantees, the head suggests that we stop and make sure that we have the arithmetic correct or the formula absolutely correct. I suppose it is because it is very difficult to give absolute guarantees, and yet I do believe that when dealing with human nature we can feel more comfortable about giving assurances and guarantees. I believe that if I treat another with courtesy and respect, I will receive courtesy and respect back. I believe that if I adopt an open, participative style of management, the response will be openness, cooperation and contribution. Helping individuals get the vision, enabling them to see the horizon alongside you, opens the mind to innovation and creativity. Of course, in seeing they may not have the understanding that you have, so that is another part of developing and improvement that comes with the job of managing.

Get the vision

I have always been impressed with a story from the New Testament in the Bible, and while it is not my intention to preach, I do see great merit in this story. The setting is the Last Supper and Jesus is giving some counsel and advice to his apostles. He addresses several points of interest towards Peter and explains that the Devil has desired to have Peter to sift him as wheat. Then he tells Peter that he has prayed for him and then gives him this great admonition: 'When thou art converted, strengthen thy brethren'. We could put this in a slightly different way without altering the meaning. We could say:'Get the vision and then help those you work with get the vision'.

If every manager could accept that same admonition, i.e. get the vision, and communicate it to all those whom they work with, I believe that performance, productivity, loyalty, commitment, teamwork, cooperation and communication would all move forward in leaps and bounds. We would create an environment where individuals would see their contribution in terms of the overall objective. They would not be planing wood or cutting planks, they would be building a ship. They would not be concerned with preserving empires which are no more than uncooperative and uncomunicative departments, they would concern themselves with the organisation as a whole. There would be a free movement of personnel across the company to get the right person doing the right job; hierarchy would be in the mind rather than in the organisation. The biggest obstacle to that happening in your organisation is believing that it can be done. Once we admit that something can be done the options become many and exciting, and what was a negative with little or no choices becomes the positive with many choices.

So far I have referred only loosely to the fact that communication should be up and down in the sharing of the vision. Only when there is a free exchange of ideas and input, can anyone really make a qualitative judgement as to the way ahead. Having the 'big picture' or getting the vision is more than some great idea that appeals to the emotions but cannot match reality. At the same time it does involve having a belief in the company, its workforce and not being a slave to restrictive thinking or practice. I suppose I am saying that to have vision one must have faith in the people who will make it happen and one must appreciate that personal, physical and mental restrictions have to be expanded in order for us to reach up and excel. I do believe that in many instances it is as simple as saying 'I can' rather than saying 'I cannot'. It also means that to get this faith in the workforce, frequent informal visits are a must. When any executive walks through the company visiting and listening, showing an interest and communicating the vision, this provides the ideal environment in which two-way communication thrives, and innovation and creativity excels. There are a number of modern stories of success that illustrate how failing companies were turned around by insightful owners and executives who went down to the shop floor to communicate. Once there they listened, invited suggestions, put across ideas and changed their minds when they could see that others knew better, and by working together they not only saved companies from bankruptcy but also turned them round into highly successful and profitable organisations.

By using an appraisal system that puts you in contact with the work force on a semi-formal basis at least four times each year, the opportunity for communication becomes even greater. Since the purpose for the appraisal is to develop individuals in order to meet the demands of the vision, a sense of purpose and direction prevails. Input from those who will 'make it happen' will be assured, and commitment and loyalty will be something that comes out of a workforce that enjoys what it does, and the company it does it for.

HAPPINESS IS PULLING TOGETHER – SUMMARY

■ There is an untapped resource available when information is shared

■ Vision is available to all if information is shared

■ Vision empowers the people when shared

■ Empowering people breaks down hierarchy

■ Vision used with appraisals enables succession planning

■ There are a number of reasons for using personal development appraisals

■ Two-way communication is essential in communicating the vision

■ Communication is more than sending a memo

■ Commitment and loyalty are products of sharing the vision

Index